BLOOM

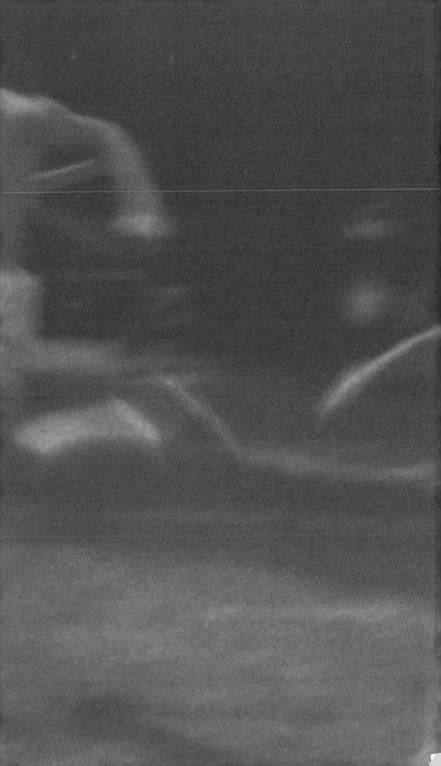

BLOOM

Queer Fiction, Art, Poetry & More

VOLUME 2, ISSUE I

SPRING 2005

BLOOM

P.O. BOX 1231
OLD CHELSEA STATION
NEW YORK, NY 10011

BLOOM is published twice a year by Arts in Bloom Project, Inc., a non-profit dedicated to queer artists, writers, and audiences. Tax-deductible donations may be made to BLOOM through our fiscal sponsor, Astraea, Inc. For more information, please contact Charles Flowers at info@bloommagazine.org or at (646) 239-9790.

EDITORIAL POLICY

BLOOM does not discriminate against the imagination. Gardeners must identify as Queer (LGBT), but the flora of their labor need not serve any pre-conceived notion of beauty. Peonies, sweet williams, ragweed, and gladiolas—every shade & shape of blossom—are all welcome. Let the garden grow.

SUBMISSION POLICY

BLOOM publishes poetry, fiction, memoir, essay, travelogue, and any other piece of writing that dazzles us. We are also pleased to present artwork that offers a fresh, sexy, startling, and/or original view of the world. Poetry: Send 3-5 poems, no more than 10 pages. Prose: Send manuscripts of 25 or fewer pages—double-spaced, of course. Art: Send a disk or slides. With all submissions, please include a SASE if you would like us to return your materials. We do not accept electronic submissions.

VISIT
www.bloommagazine.org
for more information.

ISSN 1550-3291

Printed in Canada

CONTENTS

PORTFOLIO

POETRY

Before You

I kneel down
To understand what happens. It begins
With the mouth, always

Searching toward
What takes shape, while the hand
Continues to stalk,

Small arrests are made.
Do not speak; let silence.
Light fails in this awkward place

And I am here as no one
Has ever been before:
The worst that I watch

Myself survive.
You would have me
Do this, you who are so far

From myself, who keep
Each road possible until nothing is left
To regret.

FRANK BIDART

Knot

After, no ferocity of will could the hand

•

uncurl. One day, she joked, I'll cut it off.

•

OPEN. Her hand replies that flesh insulted by being cannot bear to

•

wake. OPEN. She repeats the word to what once was hers

•

but now not.

JULIE HALL

Spring Song

Lying brittle on the surgical table
I feel the needle graze the soft epidermal hairs
rocking in their sockets,
then plunge through pink cell membrane,
reddening sheaths of fascia,
minute estuaries of the heart, piercing
the constellation of nerves in spinal orbit
to the desiccated interior of my disc.
I always thought the sky would fall,
if at all, in one swift collapse,
not like this slow narrowing
where I can still remember kissing you
and how you climbed up me
like spring clematis, greening and flowering in,
effusion of blossoms
more beautiful the longer I smelled you,
tensile and twining through,
till I nearly believe again in my life—
its unbounded striving for light—
and I'm as young as you
with your dark-water eyes and relentless body
vining up into vast currents of sky
opening, astonishingly, to receive me.

JULIE HALL

Prayer

Under a mile-thick
gray-rifted sky of lard
stuck in dirt and hoarding dark,
trees just stand and take it:
the random hurt.

Our brains forget the pain
but leave a shadow
where, say, the needle entered.
(And we collect our shadows
like a winter lake.)

You are sick now too,
and you sit, exhausted from sitting,
while I cannot stop
the fear careening between us
in wild talk,
then settling in desolate
snow drifts of silence.

From my window vigil
I watch birds eat furiously,
the way life does,
leaking thoughts on the rug
and almost touching,
the way a mind does, everything
I've lost.

In the woods I come upon
a man with a rifle cursing
at geese in his pond, and mad enough
to beat him flat to the ground
I yell at him to stop
until he does. He does stop
and walks away.

All around the trees
grip the spinning earth,
breathing their green breath
season to season, till the light falling
across my slant of sky
swims fully through me.

Today from my amphibian sleep
my hands wake warm
and carry me into the yard,
and on my knees I pull
the small wild strawberries blood red ripe
and eat them one by one.

CYNTHIA RAUSCH ALLAR

Loud Hollow Tone

It woke me in the night, the faraway sound
of my old life falling away. Of distance
growing, the rumble of tires on concrete, the jingle
and click of phones unanswered. The hiss of friends
leaving. Silence. It broke into sleep, absence
a noise, like an old friend's voice predicting doom
for me and my lover, and the murmur under
the augury, echo from her own story—
I knew quite young that I was gay.
To her, my mid-life awakening rings wrong,
condemning me in a loud hollow tone.
The old life crumbling, the friends this time, but soon
the family, shock of subsonic thunder,
of vibration so deep it cracks the bones.

ALFRED CORN

Chestnuts Roasting

1960–1970

A turn   a sigh   I'd pull into the driveway

At supper the bibled iron of his voice
Joshing its way into some slantwise judgment

Candles never lit save in December
Starring her eyes with double pilot lights

The desserts of childhood fruitcake lemon pie
A coconut and orange salad called ambrosia

Eternal life by angels heralded   by ringing jingles
Rudolf meanwhile blackballed from all reindeer

Games   why   because he had this scarlet nose

It was nothing like my room at home, a room I'd taken to redecorating almost monthly, setting a kerosene lamp on my study desk to create a colonial effect, or hanging wooden chimes from the ceiling light to make the room look Japanese. This room would bear no changes; this was a room that was meant to change me.

RICHARD McCANN

The Diarist

ERE'S ONE THING I remember, from all the things I never wrote down in my diary the summer I was eleven, the summer before my father died:

I was standing at the kitchen window, watching my brother, Davis, help our father load our station wagon with the gear we'd need to bring along—fishing rods and tackle boxes, canned foods and cooking pots, butterfly nets and BB rifles—when we left the next morning for Lumber Run, Pennsylvania, population 231. Lumber Run was paradise, my father said.

In fact, although Lumber Run had once been a boomtown, back when it still served the logging trains that once ran through there, from Williamsport to Wellsboro, it was now little more than a crossroads on Route 414, marked only by a general store, an abandoned Quonset hut, and a tar-papered tavern called the Wagon Wheel. But for two weeks each August, our father rented us a place there, an old farmhouse a former army buddy owned, wedged between the railway tracks and the banks of Pine Creek, where he liked to go fishing. He said Lumber Run reminded him of Bishop, the coal-mining town where he'd grown up, before his brakeman father was killed in a machine accident in a switching yard outside Altoona.

I knew I should have been helping my father, like Davis, as he packed our stuff into the storage space he'd created by folding down the station wagon's middle seat, so that everything was fitted neatly together. And I knew this: I didn't want to go to Lumber Run, not this time, now that I knew my mother wasn't coming with us, as she always had before. She'd already left the previous morning on the train from Silver Spring, Maryland, where we lived, to New York City, where she was going to visit her sister, who still lived in their family brownstone in Brooklyn. It was the same trip she'd taken at least monthly the whole year before, back when her mother was dying.

I dreaded my mother's departures, those Friday afternoons I came home from school to find my her in her bedroom, packing her monogrammed train case—"I like to travel light," she said. I sat on the edge of her bed as she packed, watching her reflection in the small mirror secured to the satiny lining of the train case lid; together, we seemed one instrument, the mirror and I, catching the bright flutter of my mother's dress as she crossed the bedroom, back and forth, from her dresser to her closet to her vanity.

But this time she had packed the matching Samsonites she'd bought at Woodward and Lothrop a few weeks before—a splurge from her inheritance, she said. From where I stood, I could see she wasn't traveling light. She asked if I'd please set her hatbox by the front door so she wouldn't forget it when the taxi came to take her to the station.

"I want to come with you," I told her.

She kept on packing as if she hadn't heard me.

"I've gone with you before," I urged. It was true. Once she had taken me with her for the weekend. We'd seen the Rockettes at Radio City Music Hall, and afterward we'd eaten at Schrafft's. "We'll be having the chicken à la king," she'd instructed the waitress without even consulting her menu. This proved she had once lived in New York City.

For a moment, she looked up. "No," she said. "You have to go with your father. He and I have already discussed that."

Then she resumed her work, folding her blouses into a suitcase, separating each layer with a sheet of white tissue.

A T WHAT POINT did I begin lying to my father, stammering nervous answers to whatever questions he asked me? "What are you
doing?" he asked when he came in from packing the car to find me
still standing in the kitchen.

"Making sandwiches," I told him. As I spoke, I wondered if he
believed me, since he could see quite clearly for himself that I hadn't
done anything, at least not yet—I hadn't even taken the bread from
the refrigerator. My mother had always made our sandwiches for car
trips; she liked to cut them into quarters before wrapping them in
waxed paper.

"I want you to go to Wheaton Plaza with Davis," he told me. He
said he was giving us each an extra buck, so we could stock up on
candy for the car ride.

Davis was waiting for me on the front stoop, holding the zippered
change purse in which he stored his allowance. We headed for the
plaza, through the woods behind the elementary school and across
the divided highway. On the way, Davis told me our father had
promised him he could sit in the front seat and navigate the whole
way to Lumber Run.

"I don't believe you," I said.

"It's true," Davis answered.

When we got to Wheaton Plaza, we decided to separate, as we
usually did. He went to Kahan's Hobby Shop to look at model cars;
I went to S. S. Kresge to browse the bargain bins, where I sometimes
found things, like scented bath salts or clip-on daisy earrings, that I
could present to my mother.

It was there, standing near the bargain bins, that I first noticed the
diary. It was bright pink and beautiful.

I lifted it from the rack to examine it. On its laminated cover, a
teenage girl with a ponytail was lying on her back with her legs
upraised, as if she were admiring the way she had her ankles crossed,
while chatting on her blue Princess phone. She was wearing capri
pants with a matching top. But because the picture included neither
the bed she was supposedly lying on nor the wall on which her feet

were supposedly propped, she appeared to be floating in space, in defiance of all gravity.

I knew right then I had to make it mine.

"That's a *girl's* diary," Davis said when he joined me at the S. S. Kresge lunch counter, where we'd agreed to meet, and where, having already ordered a glass of ice water, I now sat daubing a moistened paper napkin at the sticky blemish the price tag had left on the diary's plasticized cover. Having just spent ten minutes negotiating my purchase—lifting the diary casually from its display rack and saying loudly to no one in particular, "I'll bet my sister will *love* this," then presenting it the cashier and asking if it could be gift wrapped— I was still rocketing through the ionosphere of my anxiety, light-headed from the deoxygenated air.

But when Davis sat down, I felt something heavy and immutable settling beside me. I dropped the diary back into its paper sack and heard it land with a heavy thump, as if its cover girl had herself just fallen from orbit.

"It's the only kind they've got," I told him.

I couldn't tell if Davis knew that I was lying. I started to add that Mrs. Tucker, my sixth-grade teacher, had once advised our class that we should all keep diaries, especially now that we were entering junior high, so we could look back one day at all the interesting things that happened in our lives. But as soon as I started to say this, I regretted it, remembering how my father had once told me that it was easy to spot a liar, because a liar always said more than he needed to.

"Sure," Davis said. "Like you've got something to write about."

I didn't know what to say. It was true I seldom had the urge to write things down, except occasionally, when I was angry. Once I had scrawled "I HATE DAVIS" on the notepad my mother kept by the kitchen phone, though as soon as I realized that my parents would see it, I tore off the top page and ripped it into shreds, so that all that remained was the clean white page beneath, on which my secret words were still almost invisibly imprinted.

Walking back from Wheaton Plaza, I tried to think of a way to make Davis promise not to tell about the diary; I considered telling him our parents had confided in me that they were worried about the bad grades he kept getting in school—maybe that would shut him up. But when we got to our block, I realized I should be worrying even more about what I'd say to my father if he asked to see what was inside the paper bag I was carrying. All summer he'd been telling me that I needed to stop playing so much with the neighborhood girls, and once, when he overheard me gossiping on the extension phone with my best friend, Denny, he warned me, "You don't need to be a Chatty Cathy."

But I was in luck. As we got close to our house, I saw my father standing in our backyard, talking to a next-door neighbor. I went to my room and stashed the diary in my duffel bag, tucking it beneath my shorts and T-shirts. All night, I thought of it there, secured in its dark enclosure, while I lay awake, trying to imagine what I'd soon be writing on its lined pages. I tried for a long time; but I kept thinking instead of the diary my mother had kept in high school, the one she sometimes shared with me on rainy afternoons, lifting it carefully from the bottom drawer of her dresser, a small book bound in red tooled leather, with the word DIARY filigreed in gold on its cover. It was made in Morocco, she'd once told me.

"Read to me," I asked as she thumbed through the diary's fragile onionskin pages, pausing occasionally to read a passage aloud. In one, she recounted a date with a boy from Brooklyn Prep with whom she'd seen *Their Own Desire,* with Norma Shearer; in another, she described her evening at the Emerald Ball in the Grand Ballroom of the Waldorf-Astoria, hosted by the Diocese of Brooklyn. She hadn't even made it across the Waldorf's lobby, she noted, before a half-dozen suitors had filled her dance card. She had worn a polished satin gown, pale yellow, with an Empire waist.

THE NEXT DAY, Davis and I took turns as navigators, with one of us sitting in the front seat beside our father while the other sat in the rear. I sat in front first, plotting our route from home to Harrisburg, where we crossed the Susquehanna. The whole way, my father kept inventing games for him and me to play, like the one where we tried to tell which drivers were Catholics, like we were, by checking whether or not they had rosaries hanging from their rearview mirrors or plastic Virgins mounted on their dashboards, as we did. When we passed Burma Shave signs posted along the highway, we read them aloud together: NO LADY LIKES / TO DANCE OR DINE / ACCOMPA-NIED BY / A PORCUPINE / BURMA SHAVE / BURMA SHAVE. I knew even then, I suppose, that I belonged to my mother, just as Davis was our father's, but that morning, riding in the car beside him, I could remember times when I'd belonged to my father, too, sitting with him in the bathtub as a small child, while he rinsed my back with warm, soapy water, or leaning against him on the sofa on Saturday nights, watching *Have Gun, Will Travel.*

After lunch, Davis and I changed places. I sat in back, listening to my father play the same games with Davis he'd just played with me. After a while, I shut my eyes and tried to imagine what my mother was doing—perhaps she was sitting at the kitchen table in Brooklyn at that very moment, I thought, drinking sugared coffee with her sister. As soon as I pictured it, it seemed like something I might want to set down in my diary, although written from the perspective of my sitting at the table with them.

When I opened my eyes, I saw that we were passing through Sunbury, where we'd stopped the previous summer, at my insistence, to visit a snake farm I'd seen touted for miles on garish billboards. But as soon as the guide had shown us the first chicken-wire cage of timber rattlers massed horribly together, I'd gotten sick and had been forced to wait with my mother in the gift shop, looking at souvenir teacups, while Davis completed the tour with our father.

After Sunbury, the road narrowed and the small towns grew smaller yet. I knelt on the backseat, looking out the rear window, so that I saw the names of towns only after we passed through them, catching sight of signs meant to welcome arriving travelers—Dewart, Duboistown, Larryville, Avis. All afternoon, we drove deeper and deeper into my father's world, through quick tableaux of thick-waisted women draping their laundry on porch rails and teenagers huddling on the roadsides, tossing rocks at telephone poles. I'd been to places like these, the times my father took us to Bishop, where his sister still lived with her husband on a truck farm at the edge of town, past the coal mines. To get there, we had to drive by the boney dumps, the worthless mounds of slate and low-grade coal that the mining companies had rejected as waste. People said the boney dumps were dangerous; they could combust from compression. If even a small fire went unseen in a mound of boney, my aunt once told me, the whole thing could explode without warning.

It was after dark when we got to Lumber Run. Our father trained the station wagon's high beams on the house so he could find his way across the front porch to undo the padlock that secured the door. Then Davis and I dragged our suitcases from the car to our rooms. "I'll heat a few cans of ravioli," our father told us.

My room was the smallest in the house, tucked behind the kitchen. I'd chosen it the first time we'd come to Lumber Run because my mother had told me it reminded her of the butler's pantry where she'd played with dolls as a small girl in her family house in Brooklyn—not that *this* little house ever needed a *butler,* she added. But I had always liked my room, with its austere furnishings and theatrical severity, at least until now; I'd liked lying on the narrow bed in the late afternoons, with the door closed, studying the battered fiberboard dresser and the single small window whose green paper shade snapped up violently when touched. Sometimes I'd pretend I was staying in a room in a run-down boarding house or fleabag hotel, like the ones I'd seen in western movies. But now, as I stood there, picking at the flecks of ceiling plaster that had fallen onto the bedspread over the winter, the room seemed merely grim. It was nothing like my room at home, a room I'd taken to redecorating almost monthly, setting a kerosene lamp on my study desk to create a colonial effect, or hanging wooden wind chimes from the ceiling light to make the room look Japanese. This room would bear no changes; this was a room that was meant to change me.

I opened my suitcase and pulled the diary from beneath my shorts and T-shirts; then I sat down on the bed, holding it in my lap. For a while, I just stared at it, as if I were expecting it somehow to speak, although that was really stupid—I knew that. It was a diary; I was supposed to be speaking to it. But I could feel a muteness settling in my throat, as if something mangled were lodged there, and the longer I studied the diary, the more I could see how cheap it really looked, at least beneath the harsh, naked bulb of the ceiling light. For the first time, I saw how a few pages were already coming unglued from its binding, and how a crease had begun to deform the flimsy, plasticized cover. Even the cover girl looked sort of pathetic, now that I could see that the yellow of her ponytail had been printed somewhat out of register. It's not *my* fault, I wanted suddenly to explain to someone—it was the room's fault, or my father's, or my mother's, for not coming with us. Right then, I hated the diary. I wanted to hurl it to the floor and step on it.

"Time for supper!" I heard my father call out.

When I came into the kitchen, I saw that he looked happy, spooning ravioli onto paper plates. He was humming along to some song playing on the transistor radio propped on the windowsill.

"Hungry enough to eat a horse?" he asked me.

Then Davis came in and joined us. As we ate, our father kept telling us how he'd soon be catching plenty of blue trout for our suppers. "Me, too," Davis told him.

I was silent. It felt wrong, sitting there beside the empty seat that belonged to my mother. I wondered if maybe she was having her supper then, too, or if she'd gone someplace, like to a movie with her sister. As I imagined my mother, I began feeling bad about having wanted to hurt my own diary.

As soon as my father finished his meal, he carried his paper plate across the kitchen and stuffed it into the garbage. "Let's have some fun," he said to Davis and me.

"Like what?" Davis asked him.

I looked at my father. I thought maybe he wanted to take us to the Wagon Wheel—he and our mother had often liked going there at night to drink beer, the two of them sitting on stools at the pine-paneled bar while Davis and I fed nickels to the jukebox, playing "The Wayward Wind" over and over, because our mother said she liked it. Or maybe he just wanted to take us out back to practice shooting tin cans with our Daisy BB rifles, as he'd taught us on a weekend camping trip a few months before. He'd gotten us the rifles for Christmas.

"I thought we'd head down to the railroad tracks," he said.

I liked walking to the tracks with my father. More than once he'd told Davis and me the tracks made him think of his father, who must have passed through Lumber Run at least a few times, or so he imagined, on freights hauling coal.

Davis and I went to change into our sneakers and then joined our father in the backyard, where he was waiting with his flashlight. We followed him across the cut grass and through a small arcade of trees, toward the watchman's shanty, where highway crews stored salt for winter roads now that trains no longer stopped there.

"Quiet," he said when we got to the railway crossing. He bent down toward the tracks, as he did each time he brought us here, pretending to be listening for the distant sound of the freight train on which his father had long ago ridden.

"Can you hear it?" he asked.

Davis and I just stood there in silence, watching him. Nothing was coming. For a moment, I tried to imagine my father as he must have been as a boy growing up in Bishop, though it was hard to do so, since he spoke so seldom of his childhood, except to say he'd had to go to work when he was ten, sweeping out railway cars, and that when he was twelve, he'd been consigned for a year to the State Youth Sanatorium for Tuberculosis. Once he had told us that when he was a small boy, his father had called him "honey."

He stepped into the railway bed, almost slipping on the oily gravel. Davis and I moved toward him. I couldn't believe how dark it was, though when I looked up I saw the Dog Star quietly blazing above me. "It's called Sirius," my mother had once told me when we were sitting together in our backyard on a summer night a few years before.

"Here you go," our father said as he reached into one of his trouser pockets. He withdrew a fistful of coins, from which he counted out the pennies. Then Davis and I laid the pennies on the tracks, one by one, knowing that when we returned the next morning, we'd find them flattened and flung into the high weeds by night trains we'd neither seen nor heard as we slept.

THE NEXT MORNING, I watched my father head down the narrow path to Pine Creek, his fishing rod and tackle box in one hand, his creel slung over his shoulder, beating on his back as he walked. I was sitting on the front steps, eating my cereal.

"Don't you want to come?" he'd asked as he was leaving.

"Not right now," I'd told him. I'd said I'd try to catch up later, after I'd done the dishes.

I watched him walk away until he disappeared behind a stand of cattails; then I carried my bowl back to the house. I was relieved not to have gone with him to Pine Creek, where he would have once again instructed me how best to bait my hook. I hated touching the worms, with their greasy, quivering bodies, as I pulled them from the bait bucket, and I hated jabbing them onto the barbed hooks, making sure I'd stuck each of them onto the hook in at least two places, so it wouldn't fall off too quickly in the water.

The house was silent when I entered it. Davis had already left earlier that morning; I didn't know where he'd gone. But that was all right. I liked being alone with no one around to see me. The whole past year, I'd begun feigning illness on school days so I could stay home by myself. Once my parents had left for work, I'd lie for hours on the basement sofa, slowly devouring the coffee cakes I made for myself from Bisquick, brown sugar, and margarine, until I could feel myself at long last dissolving—nameless, benumbed, unfettered—into the noise and canned laughter of the game shows I watched on TV.

But now I had something important to do. I went into my room and retrieved the diary from the drawer where I'd hidden it the night before. I was glad to see it looked a lot better by daylight; even the cover girl looked brighter and more cheerful. I carried it out to the front porch glider, along with a pencil I'd found in a kitchen drawer. If someone showed up, I figured, I could slip it quickly beneath a cushion.

But when I sat down and opened the diary—I was ready to inscribe my first entry—I was jarred by the emptiness of its white ruled pages. What was I supposed to write there? The only thing I could think of was the odd, throbbing absence of my mother, and how the previous summer I'd sat beside her on the very same glider, reading the *Reader's Digest* condensed books I'd found in the attic, while she flipped through back issues of fashion magazines, occasionally pausing to comment on a pair of shoes or a cocktail dress she particularly admired. But that wasn't something I could put in my diary. What would be the point of that? It was stupid—*case closed.*

Maybe if I just got a bite to eat, I thought, I might calm down. I went inside to get a piece of bread from the loaf on the kitchen counter. I ate the bread quickly, standing there; then I ate another slice, and then another, and then another one yet. Then I saw how much bread I had eaten and worried that my father would be upset with me for eating so much, but that didn't stop me—I couldn't seem to help myself. I laid a slice on the counter and rolled it around until it turned back into dough, and then I ate that, too, because it was sweeter like that, almost like candy.

By the time I got back to the porch glider, I felt sluggish. I told myself I should lie down, since I felt too tired to write, even though I could feel something hard and insistent tugging inside me, telling me I should try to put at least something on paper, even if it was something I invented, since I wasn't sure I could think of anything true to say. I opened the diary to try again, but I felt even worse, just from holding it. Maybe I'd thrown away my money by buying it. Maybe I'd made a terrible mistake. What if I needed my money for something else?

That's when I heard Davis come into the house through the back door, laughing and talking with someone whose voice I didn't recognize. I hurriedly shoved the diary beneath one of the glider cushions, then went into the house.

"Dad's looking for you," Davis said when I came into the kitchen, where he was standing with his friend Frank, a local boy he'd met while fishing the previous summer. After their initial meeting, they'd gone out hiking together almost every afternoon, canteens strapped to their army surplus belts, while I went to country auctions in the car with my mother, who was trying to add to her collection of cut glass.

I could see Frank didn't much like me—or maybe he was just shy, as I'd once heard Davis telling our father. In any case, Frank barely looked in my direction as Davis told me all about the morning they'd spent together—how they'd gone to the tracks to gather the flattened pennies, as he and I had planned to do, and how they had then walked to the remains of the old sawmill with BB rifles to shoot at some black snakes Frank's brother said he had seen there. Now they were packing a bag lunch, Davis said, to bring to our father.

I didn't need to ask if the BB rifle Frank had used had in fact been mine; I could see it sitting right there in the corner, propped against the wall.

"See you," Frank murmured in my direction as they left.

I was alone again, and I wasn't sure what to do with myself. I didn't want to resume my diary. I didn't want to read a book. There was nothing good to eat in the house except the loaf of bread, from which I'd already eaten too much. For a moment, I was sorry they hadn't asked me to come with them.

That's when I decided to follow them down the path toward Pine Creek. At first, I couldn't hear them ahead of me, not even when I stopped in the first clearing in the cattails, where people sometimes dumped their old tires. But by the time I got to the second clearing— someone had abandoned an old car there, I noticed, a broken-down junker with its running boards nearly rusted out—I could hear them laughing. I stepped into the cattails. From there, I could see them sitting side by side at the edge of Pine Creek, talking back and forth between themselves as they took off their shoes and socks and rolled up the legs of their blue jeans. They stepped into the water—neither seemed shocked by its sudden coldness—and began wading toward the rock where our father sat fishing.

Then I saw Davis start to slip on the creek's mossy stone bottom. I could see small whirlpools of white water clutching at his ankles, and a look of panic rising in his face. I wondered if Frank could see the panic, too.

For a moment, I thought to call out to warn my brother, suddenly remembering the times he and I had played there together, building small dams from branches and twigs and then coming back later to kick them apart.

But I stayed silent.

Davis slipped; Frank caught him. Frank laughed, and Davis splashed him water. Then they continued wading toward our father, Davis holding the paper lunch sack above his head, the way a soldier carries his rifle through high water.

I stepped forward from the edge of the cattails. But when I emerged into the open, I saw that my father was watching me.

He waved. I waved, my hand stirring from the cattails a sudden updraft made visible my gnats. But I went no farther. I wasn't sure if I was waving hello or good-bye.

WHAT MIGHT I have written about my father in my diary, had I been able to write down anything at all? That I felt afraid when he watched me too long or too closely? Or that the things he kept warning me to stop doing, like cutting out the Winnie Winkle fashion paper dolls from the Sunday funnies or designing elaborate ball gowns for my favorite movie stars, were in fact the very things that came most naturally, unbidden, from my hand? *If thy right hand offend thee, cut it off.* Or maybe I would simply have written that I loved him, and missed him, and that I wanted him to call me "honey," too, as his father had called him.

In any case, I was unable to write even a word. Not one word the whole time.

Each morning for the next three days, as soon as I was alone in the house, I resumed my seat on the porch glider, my pencil poised, my diary opened on my lap, waiting for words to strike. One morning it occurred to me I could address the whole diary to my mother, making her a record of all the things I'd done since I'd last seen her, though in my heart I knew I'd done nothing worth writing down. Another time, I decided I should save the diary to use later, after I'd begun what I hoped would one day become my real life, a life just like the one my mother described herself as having once had, catching a taxi to the Stork Club for cocktails before grabbing a late supper at Luchow's or Toots Shor's.

But for the most part, I just sat there until I felt too lonely to persist. Then I wandered over to the general store to buy red licorice and pretzel rods, counting and recounting my coins, worried that I was depleting my savings too quickly; or I walked the railroad tracks across the old wooden trestle, staring down into the depths below, which I could see through gaps in the cross ties. I carried the diary with me, tucked into my waistband and covered by my camp shirt. But the diary sometimes chafed me as I walked, and when this happened, I'd be seized by the sudden desire to throw it onto the tracks, even though that same desire filled me at once with shame, as if I'd just caught myself wanting to kill something small and defenseless. Once, on my way home from one of my walks, I ran into Mrs. Purvis, a widow I'd met with my mother at an auction the previous summer. She invited me back to her house, where we sat on her porch, drinking sweet tea while she showed me an old scrapbook filled with photos of her and her dead husband. When I stood to leave, I decided I wanted to show her the diary, though I told her I'd just found it on the side of the road. "I don't know," she said as she examined it. "It looks mighty new to me."

As for my father: I knew he was upset with me. Each late afternoon, when he got home from fishing, he came to my room and stood in the doorway, as if there was something he wanted to say to me. But I just kept on reading, stretched out on my bed, its coarse woolen blanket tucked tight into army corners, as he had taught me. After he turned and walked away, I shut the book and listened to him as he crossed the kitchen to the sink. I could hear him turn on the tap, and I could hear the water rushing forward as he began to gut and clean whatever trout he'd caught that day.

But on the fourth afternoon, he got angry.

When I got home from walking the railroad tracks, I found him in the backyard, watering the lawn with a garden hose, as he sometimes did, so that he could come back later and hunt for night crawlers, which emerged when the soil was wet.

"I want you to tell me what's going on," he said as soon as he saw me.

"What do you mean?" I asked, worried that he'd somehow found the diary, even though I felt sure I had it with me, tucked into my waistband. I had to fight the urge to reassure myself by touching it.

"You haven't come fishing like I've asked," he said, looking at me directly.

"But I'm going to," I told him.

"Sure," he said. "When?"

"I will."

"So you say," he said.

I just stood there, shifting from foot to foot. Had he been like my mother, I might have distracted him by getting him to tell me some story about himself, but that didn't work with him.

At supper, Davis started talking about an abandoned CCC camp he'd come across while hiking up a fire trail with Frank; they'd seen the remains of a few barracks and a tree growing through what they figured had once been the floor of the mess hall. Our father said the whole country should still be thanking FDR for the CCC and the New Deal, because without him no one would have gotten even an honest dollar for an honest day's work.

As soon as I had finished eating, I excused myself. I couldn't stop thinking about my diary. Even though I knew I'd returned it to its drawer the second I'd gotten back into the house, I needed to check to make sure it was there, the same way my mother sometimes had to turn the car around and drive home, worried that she'd left a cigarette burning and that it had already fallen onto the carpet.

But I was also nervous about going back into my room, since I didn't want to do anything that would call attention to myself. So I went out back to catch lightning bugs, just like normal. A few minutes later, Davis came out the kitchen door and settled himself in a chair beneath the back porch light, looking through a copy of *Boys' Life* he'd gotten from Frank. He and Frank liked reading *Boys' Life* together, mesmerizing themselves with stories of scouts who proved quick-minded in the midst of disaster, slashing open a snakebite puncture on a child's arm to suck the venom out or forming a human chain to rescue a skater who'd fallen through thin ice.

I liked catching lightning bugs; I liked collecting them in jars with lids I'd studded with air holes. At night, the jars made small, radiant galaxies that by morning would be dead.

I went to the honeysuckle bushes in the side yard, where the lightning bugs were flickering among the fragrant white and yellow flowers;

I reached out a hand and grabbed one from where it hovered, flashing, in midair. Then I remembered a trick a girl had once told me about in school. If you pulled off a lightning bug's belly, she said, and stuck it on your finger, you could make a ring from it, because when a lightning bug died, its belly continued to glow.

I wasn't sure I could actually do it, but I gave it my full attention, first pulling the wings from the lightning bug's body, then setting its belly, still glowing, on my left ring finger. If I squinted, I realized, the lightning bug's luminescent belly looked almost like the yellow diamond solitaire my mother had inherited after her mother's death. But who would inherit the solitaire, I wondered, when my mother died? It would never go to a boy.

I looked up and saw Davis still reading beneath the porch light. I walked across the yard toward him, holding my left hand as steady as possible.

"Look," I said, showing him what I had made.

He looked up briefly from his magazine and gazed at my finger. "That's dumb," he said.

"No," I said. "It's beautiful."

Then I heard the screen door slam, and when I looked up, I saw my father coming out to the porch from the kitchen. I hurriedly turned my hand over, and the lightning bug's belly dropped into the grass. For a moment, I watched as it extinguished itself like a cigarette butt's dying ember.

"What are you doing?" my father asked.

"Getting the lightning bugs something to eat," I told him. To prove it, I bent over and yanked up a few handfuls of grass to stuff into one of the jars.

"I thought maybe you boys were telling ghost stories," he said. "That's what my brothers and I used to do after dark. Did you ever hear 'The Monkey's Paw'? We always liked 'The Monkey's Paw.'"

"We saw it on TV," I told him.

"Oh," he said. Then he stepped forward from the porch into the dark. "I want you boys to help me look for night crawlers," he told us.

He instructed Davis to go around to the front porch and fetch a few flashlights and the dirt-filled coffee can in which he kept his live bait. When Davis left, he turned toward me. "Maybe you won't mind helping with *this*," he said. "Since you can't seem to find it within yourself to come fishing, I mean."

"I want to help," I told him, though it wasn't true. I hated searching for night crawlers. I hated having to grasp them, damp and slick, as they first emerged from the ground, and I hated the way they tore into pieces if I got nervous and pulled at them too hard or quickly.

Davis came back around the side of the house, carrying the bait can, along with two flashlights, which he was toting in his pant pockets. He had switched on a third flashlight and was holding it under his chin as he walked, so that his illuminated face looked cadaverous and ghoulish. "Ooooohh," he was moaning like a ghost as he came toward us, "you've got three wishes on the monkey's paw . . ."

"Okay, that's enough," our father said. "Let's get down to business."

For a moment, I stood there without moving, as if Davis's words had cast some spell that had stilled me. I knew what my wish would be, if one wish were granted me: *Please let me seem, even if only for this hour, my father's son.* I knew the time had come. I knew I had to please him.

Then I heard my own voice speaking, a muffled sound, as if from a distance: "Dad," I was saying, "I'll go search in the compost."

I could see my father was surprised by what I'd said, just as I was. He knew I was afraid of the compost pile. It sat in the darkest and farthest part of the yard, near the stand of trees that separated our house from the Wagon Wheel's parking lot. Davis and Frank had once told me that rats went to feed there, drawn by the stench of decomposition; they said brown snakes liked to nest there, seeking the warmth that rises from decay. But it was also where night crawlers were most abundant. I knew that.

"Are you sure?" my father asked.

"It's not fair," Davis complained. "Dad said he wanted us to do this *together.*"

"Yes, I'm sure," I told my father.

"All right," he said.

He handed me a flashlight and I started to walk away.

"Wait," he said. He removed his fishing cap, the one to which he affixed his hand-tied flies, and set it on my head. "Walk softly," he told me. "Keep your eyes peeled."

I crossed the yard, walking softly. I kept my eyes peeled.

When I got to the compost, I stepped over the low chicken-wire fencing that enclosed it, sinking to my ankles in soft mulch. I guided my flashlight's beam back and forth across the surface. Everywhere the light fell, I saw small, sudden motions: a wood spider struggling through the sticky albumen glazing an eggshell; pale grubs devouring wet leaves. Then I heard music, the faint sound of a song playing on the jukebox at the Wagon Wheel. It was hard not to think of my mother, to picture her sitting at the bar in her white sundress with the spaghetti straps, holding her beer glass aloft. "Meet my pretty wife," my father would say, introducing her to his fisherman friends— "Meet my wife, pretty Maria."

I looked up. On the other side of the yard, my father was holding a flashlight for Davis, who was kneeling within the wide circumference of its beam. Davis was lowering his hand toward the ground and pulling up a night crawler.

I wanted my father to watch me. I knelt in the compost and reached down, and all at once, I saw at least a dozen night crawlers emerging simultaneously from their air holes, as if in response to a single command. I was just beginning to touch one, preparing to yank it out from its hole, when suddenly something fell toward me—a leaf?—and landed on my shoulder.

I turned to look: Its wings struck my face. Whatever it was, it was caught in the fabric of my shirt, straining to pull itself free. It jerked upward and rose briefly, only to catch itself again on my collar. I could feel the violence and terror of its movement at my throat, thrashing and thrashing.

"Get it off me!" I cried.

My father came running, his flashlight's beam swinging crazily through the dark, like an emergency.

"Get it off me!" I begged him. "Get it off!"

He pointed the flashlight at my collar, where the creature was struggling, its pale green wings furiously beating.

Through the flashlight's beam, I could see my father study me; I saw how I looked in his eyes.

"It's a luna moth," he said. He reached toward my collar and flicked it with his fingertips. Suddenly it seemed small and insufficient. It rose and flew away.

"I thought you'd been bitten by a snake," he said.

"Me, too," I said. "That's what I thought, too." We both knew I was lying.

"Just get inside," he muttered.

I switched off my flashlight and walked back across the yard. As I passed Davis, he whispered dramatically, "Oooohh, it's the curse of the monkey's paw."

I said nothing back. When I got to the porch, I didn't turn around to look at my father.

I simply opened the back door and stepped into the kitchen, flinching from the sudden brightness of the ceiling light. When my eyes adjusted, I saw it. I saw it lying right there on the kitchen table. My diary. Someone had found it and taken it from my dresser, and now it was lying there, just lying there, out in the open, beside the salt and pepper shakers.

THAT NIGHT, I didn't claim the diary by taking it back to my room; in fact, I didn't even want to touch it. I went right to bed and stayed there until late the next morning, when I heard my father drive off in the station wagon, headed to Slate Run, where he was planning to try his hand at fly-fishing with some men he'd met at the Wagon Wheel.

When I got up for breakfast, the diary was still sitting in the center of the table. I just sat there looking at it as I ate my cereal, imagining the things I might have written down had I gone to New York with my mother. Perhaps we would have had dinner at Michel's, my mother's favorite restaurant in Park Slope, or perhaps we would have taken in an early movie at the Rialto. Perhaps I would have been happy simply to sit in the Victorian room my grandmother had called her "boudoir," remembering the time she had invited me in to ask me questions for a personality quiz she'd prepared on a legal pad especially for me. "Whom do you prefer," she had asked, "Jayne Mansfield or Marilyn Monroe? Whom do you regard as the greater actress, Bette Davis or Greta Garbo? Which do you prefer, the plain Hershey bar or the Hershey with almonds?"

I sat at the kitchen table most of the morning, as if I were bidding the diary adieu. But I couldn't sit there forever. I had something to do, something I'd figured out the night before while lying awake in my room.

I waited until I finished lunch. Then I stacked my dishes in the sink and went to the broom closet, where my father stored our Daisy BB rifles, out of immediate reach. I took my rifle and carried it out to the front porch glider. Then I began to clean it, just as my father had taught me, first moistening a cleaning patch with a few drops of heavy oil, then inserting the patch directly into the muzzle on a long rod in order to swab the bore. When I was done, I opened the small paper cylinder of BBs and poured them into my palm; I fed the BBs slowly into the narrow loading tube affixed to the base of the barrel.

I carried the loaded rifle down the path toward Pine Creek, past the first clearing and through the cattails. At the second clearing, I stopped. I pulled hard on the cocking lever and raised the rifle straight, positioning the old junked car in its sight.

I fired. The first shot struck the junker's windshield. I pressed the trigger again so that a second shot struck the glass, and when I saw that my aim was right and good, I pulled the trigger over and over, until the windshield cracked into a silvery web and then shattered, raining small bits of glass across the dashboard. I liked the way it felt. I walked around to the driver's side and shot out those windows, too, and then I shot at the side panel until it was scored and dimpled, and then I walked around to the other side and did the whole thing over again. Finally, I took aim at the small winged ornament on the rusty hood. But I wasn't through.

I set the rifle down walked back to the house empty-handed. Once there, I took the diary from the kitchen table and carried it back down to clearing. I opened one of the car doors and set the diary on the front seat, and then backed up until I had the cover girl within my rifle's sight. I fired at her, too, again and again, until she and the diary were both obliterated, the pink plastic cover split from its cardboard backing, the blank pages shredded.

Later, I ate supper with Davis. We heated up two more cans of ravioli, since our father had warned us he'd be late—he was stopping at the Wagon Wheel to drink some beer with his buddies. After supper, I went into the front room to wait on the musty horsehair sofa. I was eager to tell my father how I had practiced my marksmanship, as he had encouraged.

I heard him on the porch before he came in. From the way he grabbed at the screen door, I could tell he was angry. "Where are you?" he called out as he came into the house. He was calling my name.

I was scared. The room was dark. It was late. "I'm here," I finally said.

Suddenly my father was standing in the doorway. "What the hell did you think you were doing?" he demanded. "What the hell made you think you could destroy something that isn't even yours?"

I knew what I thought I was doing: I was trying to please him. Even now, looking back, I honestly believe that. But what could I have said to him then? That I had hoped to turn myself into a son he might love?

My silence made him angrier. "That damn car isn't yours!" he bellowed. He said the car belonged to one of the bartenders at the Wagon Wheel. It wasn't a junker. It ran just fine. He said he was just drinking a beer and minding his own damn business when some man he'd never even met before came into the bar and told him what I had done, how I'd been down at the creek shooting at a car until I'd destroyed it. "And just how the hell do you think you're going to pay *that* back?" he asked.

I could see he was trying to contain himself, even though he was furious. I just listened to him yell. After a while, he started to spend himself until, finally, he just stood there in silence. It wasn't until then that he noticed that the room he was standing in was dark. He reached over and switched on the table lamp.

"Do you have anything to say for yourself?" he asked.

"No," I said.

"Then I want you to get ready for bed," he said. "I'll go ahead and check you."

I knew what he meant: Each night in Lumber Run before Davis and I went to bed, we stood before him so he could check our bodies for ticks that we ourselves might not have spotted.

He unscrewed the shade from the table lamp next to the sofa and bent my head into the arc of light, parting my hair with his fingers as he inspected my scalp.

"Stand up," he said.

I stood. I began to undress, as I did each night: first my shoes and socks, then my pants, then my shirt, until I was standing there naked. He lifted the table lamp and moved it back and forth across my body, studying my chest, my back, my legs, my buttocks. I felt right then as if there were nothing about me that was not visible to him. I could feel the heat of the bulb on my skin.

I hate you, I thought. *I hate you, I hate you.*

In retrospect, I'm not sure who I was hating most right then, as I stood there—my father, my mother, or myself. That night I didn't know that my father would soon die suddenly of liver failure, or that it would be Davis who would one day explain to me that it was not he but Mrs. Purvis who had told my father she had seen me with a diary, or that I had scarcely even begun what was to become my life of secrets.

I knew only the heat of the bulb as it passed over my naked body. *I hate you,* I thought, *I hate you.* I no longer had a diary. But for the first time I felt as if I actually needed one, a need that was at once acute and unfamiliar. It wasn't that I needed to speak to my mother in her absence; it wasn't that I wanted to make something up. For the first time, I wanted to write something down, something true, even if I had no idea what words I'd one day use in doing so.

EMILY GROPP

O

In half-dream hours before sleep arrives, with its locks
(if you need the keys they're on the mantel)
I exhale a secondhand phrase underbreath.
My dead friend at its origins. Windbones split.
Only my translator is completely aware of what happened inside at
    that moment.
Me, I'm farther from daylight island but approaching.
They say I lie through my teeth,
the adults do behind the woodpile with the antlers.
If you want to, stay so far away and don't believe me.
If you want to, come here.

ELIZABETH BRADFIELD

Creation Myth: Periosteum and Self

> *Hormonally imbalanced females of all deer species*
> *have been known to grow antlers.*

This is what I choose. Periosteum
rampant on my brow, and testosterone
to activate it at the pedicle.

> *"Luxury organs," so called because they aren't*
> *necessary for survival.*

I choose the possibility buried
in the furrow which has ceased to disappear
between my eyes in sleep, in the skin
my lover has touched her lips to
in passion's spent lull.

> *Females produce young each year. Males produce antlers.*

Forget the in-vitro, the expensive catheter of sperm
slipped past the cervix, the long implications
of progeny. I am more suited to other sciences,
other growth.

> *Researchers have snipped bits of periosteum*
> *from pedicles, grafted them onto other parts*
> *of a buck's body, and grown antlers.*

I'll graft it to my clavicle. My cheekbone. Ankle.
Coccyx. Breast. Anywhere. At last visible,
the antler will grow, will branch. Fork
and tine. Push and splay.

> *Researchers have tricked deer into growing and*
> *casting as many as four sets of antlers in one*
> *calendar year.*

It won't wait for what's appropriate, but starts
in the subway, in the john, talking
to a friend about her sorrows, interviewing for a job.
My smooth desk, my notebook, my special pen with particular ink, my
Bach playing through the wall of another

room—not the location
of the prepared field, but what the light says, when
the light says *now*.

> *Deer literally rob their body skeletons to grow*
> *antlers they'll abandon a few months later.*

It could care less
about the inconvenience
forking from my knee, the difficulty
of dressing, embracing, or piloting a car. It doesn't care

> *Essentially bucks and bulls are slaves to their antlers.*

if I'm supposed to be paying bills or
taking the dog for her evening walk. There is no sense
to it, no logic, just thrust. It does its work.
It does its splendid, difficult, ridiculous work and then,
making room for its next, more varied rising,

gorgeous and done, it falls away.

ELIZABETH BRADFIELD

Netting

She wants so badly to catch something, net held
over a reflecting eddy. She's pulled in
jewel-eyed frogs, their toes
splayed on the canoe's smooth hull,
throats throbbing. She's captured
small snails and, once, some roe, but mostly
just bottom muck, silt, and thickening leaves. Again,

into the water lilies and duckweed, the heavy sack
of ooze deep within the net's bell, weight
unexpected as a breast's warm heft. Inside, mummichogs
and sticklebacks torque themselves and she sifts
through the black spill for shrimp. The net
bends heavy from her hand,
spills over. Reach into my chest,

into the bone sieve where I keep my heart, and this
is what you'll find. Substance black,
thick, and silken: staining the lines of your skin,
smelling potent and determined,
shot through with green ribbons of grass,
small, silver things twitching and gasping in it,
remarkable and ready in seconds to drown.

NOAH MICHELSON

A Long Line of Bad Decisions

I come from a long line of men who made
bad decisions, big things like where
to immigrate, how many children are too many children, who
to love when you no longer love your wife or simply want
a blowjob after eight hours on your feet, little things
like buying a car because it has fins, betting
next month's rent on the slowest horse, believing
a psychic when she says hurry, invest everything
you've got in plastics or someday you'll be sorry.
Some warning,
with them it was always someday
and I'm worried they've come back for what they feel
should have been theirs in the first place, I feel
them shuffling their feet under my skin, unable to make
eye contact with each other, even now, even from this
distance, the boredom and embarrassment of death
after the cigars go out, after the card tricks go wrong yet again,
no wings, no horns, these are wayward molecules, outlaw
cells conspiring, saving their money to buy as much land
from my body as they can, subdivisions and supermarkets
swelling up around every nerve, numberless new cities
with noble intentions, this sequence of infamy
reverberating, moths reverting to caterpillars,
I am condemned to live
their lives all over again: wedding bells
on the wrong day with the wrong woman walking down the aisle,
the engine running with the garage door shut, four weeks
in an empty apartment and the phone has not rung once.

AMY GROSHEK

Single Life #13: Dinner at Her Place

for M

When she takes my hand
and tries to kiss me
I'll say I'm busy,
my lips are resting,
do I hear someone
breaking into the living room.
I haven't yet finished
my wine, I'm only
halfway through *Fossils of Texas,*
I have a prearranged call
to my house
in five minutes
from China.
There is the moon, dim
in the long June dusk,
the way she drops her eyes
to her empty hands.
But I've hurt enough women
to start a commune:
just crossing the room
I stub my toes on regrets.
We could be long and deep and glorious.
We could be life's one brilliance
purchased with a thousand failures.
My cat has developed
hepatitis.
The Navy SEALs are invading.
If I don't go out
and start the engine
my truck will explode.

Remnant

Last night, I fell from a tree.
It was a dream.
It was Tuesday, I woke, a paper wasp drowning
on the night stand in a glass of water.
Spasms rippled her body until forgive me,
I call it—nothing—happened.
You were asleep.
You wouldn't even know what I'm talking about.
I wouldn't even tell you what I know.
The sound of spoons can be heard around the house.
I'm afraid, I'm happy, I love you, I want to eat.
Meanwhile, those little birds are singing
in a language strange to you & me as I watch two
workers load sealed boxes above the slaughter
of glass. The sun is cutting.
Then, in the street, a crate of oranges drops,
breaks.

MARK MOODY

Breaking the Spell

It always begins in the mix:
fat afternoons at the Eagle,
shirtless in spite of the fog
since we're already tan by May.
Everyone in boots and jeans, drunk
on beer, taunting my perversions
having licked the yellow Ducati.
Or walking in on a sunny afternoon
to find you've taken over my apartment:
stoned, queens for a day, hands full
of watermelon, spitting seeds
from my balcony, murmuring like geishas
over dark and muscled men.

But the dream trickles down
to a series of rooms fluorescent
and linoleum, where the virus
devours your supple, extravagant lives
and in the end I am standing alone
on the balcony, watching
you all fall away like
the little black seeds
on that hot August day.

Tonight I go to the well of thunder
to bathe in its bitter cathartic.
Pinned open with the click of locks
whips will crack, bolting me into the present,
changing me like light, from particle to wave.
A rippling heat will evanesce
over a cipher of carmine welts
and a sheen of glistening sweat.

Then, when the bright emptiness comes
and life is a bite of tart green apple,
I'll close my eyes
for as much and as long as I can.

She went shopping. Eve wasn't supposed to be in the department store at all. Because of the earrings. She had gotten only a bit of community service and an order not to inhabit the premises of the store for a year. Which made stepping through the glass doors when they opened at nine o'clock very exciting.

LUCY JANE BLEDSOE

The Gracemonger

This is an excerpt from The Gracemonger, *a novel about Eve Glass, once an Olympic sprinter who is now a motivational speaker and author of two self-help books:* Endurance for Achievers *and* If Grace Is the Goal. *Unfortunately, her own endurance is waning and her confidence in her expertise on grace is paling. She's in love with Audrey, a renowned poet, who feels very ambivalent about being involved with a self-help writer.*

EVE AWOKE to a lovely Saturday. The night rains had washed the sky clean, leaving only a transparent blue, and the sunlight coming in her bedroom was pure and brilliant. She could see the entire color spectrum in each ray. Eve's fever was gone, but it had left her feeling dry and empty. She got up and drank two glasses of water, and then lay in the stream of sunlight for a long time, as if it could recharge her.

A journey. That's what she needed. She would go to Audrey.

Eve leapt out of bed. She yanked her suitcase off the top shelf of her closet, threw it on the tangled sheets, and started rifling through her clothes, looking for the perfect effect. Nothing. How do you dress for a poet who cares most about the beauty of language? All of Eve's clothes looked tacky, too lacy, too short, too *some*thing. She

pulled on a low-cut white tank top, a purple miniskirt, a pair of san-
dals, and grabbed her shoulder bag.

She went shopping. Eve wasn't supposed to be in the department
store at all. Because of the earrings. She had gotten only a bit of community service and an order not to inhabit the premises of the store
for a year. Which made stepping through the glass doors when they
opened at nine o'clock very exciting. She spent several hours trying
on shoes and then leather coats, of which Audrey would never
approve, and then admonished herself to get serious. Dressing to
please someone else is a complicated business. You don't want to dress
as they do because people are rarely attracted to themselves, so you
must dress how they would dress if they had thought of it. You have
to be a step ahead of them. In the case of dressing for Audrey, she had
to be casually elegant, but the elegant part had to be disguised
because Eve doubted Audrey would want to acknowledge to herself
that she liked elegant. Though she was quite sure she did. Her poetry,
after all. Eve did find a beautiful white cotton shirt, classically cut,
quite elegant actually, but one shirt did not make an outfit.

Eve supposed she wasn't trying hard enough. She shopped aim-
lessly, wandering among the racks, in and out of departments, as if
she were a nomad hunting herbs. That very thought came to her
while she rode the escalator down from the fourth to the third floor,
and she looked out over the merchandise, like a field of wildflowers,
trying to figure which patch might yield the greatest harvest. She did,
for a moment, truly believe herself to be in the out-of-doors, perhaps
somewhere in southern Italy, perhaps a couple of thousand years ago,
her eyes alighting on some bright green that might be just the herb
for which she searched.

She returned to her real self somewhere among the dress blouses.
The department was quiet, except for one woman who wanted a
cream silk blouse to go with the chocolate brown wool slacks she was
wearing. She seemed a bit urgent about the cream blouse and had
engaged a saleslady to help her. She wanted attention, lots of it, and
that interested Eve. The woman did not want the saleslady to wander off to attend to other tasks. She wanted company as she pulled
different blouses from the racks and held them against her thin

chest. A nod or comment from the saleslady would send her to the mirror for further evaluation. Eve noticed that when she made these trips to the mirror, she left her purse on the floor by the rack from which the blouse came.

A thief has logic, just like anyone else. Eve had been banned from this place. Why? Because she had stolen from them and might again. She shouldn't have sneaked into the department store, but knowing that she would not steal from them again, which was really the issue, not her presence itself, she didn't feel guilty being there. Now, her reasoning continued, if she took this *purse,* she wouldn't be stealing from the store. She would be stealing from that lady in the chocolate brown slacks who wanted a cream blouse. But the logic went deeper than that. What she was about to do didn't feel like stealing at all. It was more like asking someone out on a date, that vertigo from the dual chance of rejection and possibility. That purse pulsed like the cover of a good novel. Eve wanted to look inside.

So she hovered, watching the purse. The woman picked it up off the floor, slung it from her elbow as she moved to another rack of blouses. The purse seemed heavy, pulling on her arm, as she pushed blouse after blouse aside in her search. Then, an interesting blouse. The arm straightened and the purse slid to her wrist. She bent and let it rest on the carpet. She held the blouse against her chest and turned to get an opinion from the saleslady. But the saleslady had wandered back to her checkout island. Which annoyed the customer. Eve saw her frown, consider whether to call across to the saleslady, and then compose herself, and finally, with the blouse held out in front her on the hanger, stride over to the checkout island.

Her purse remained on the carpet, beneath the hanging blouses.

That would have been Eve's moment. The customer's back was turned. She was absorbed in her pursuit of the saleslady's opinion. But Eve was torn. As much as she wanted to lift the purse, she was interested in what would happen now between the customer and the saleslady. She empathized with the customer. After all, there was no one else in the department other than Eve, and she wasn't asking for assistance. There was no reason the saleslady couldn't have remained in attendance.

"Too plain," Eve heard the saleslady say rather too sharply. She dropped the pile of tissue she'd been arranging and bustled to a rack in the far corner of the department. The customer followed, still carrying her tailored cream blouse. Eve's opportunity was yet improved, but still she watched as the saleslady held up a cream blouse with a big ruffle down the entire row of buttons. Now Eve wasn't a professional fashion consultant, but even she could see that that woman in her chocolate brown slacks would no more wear those ruffles than she would wear spike heels.

If, for Eve, thievery were a kind of revenge, she would have found something to steal from the snooty saleslady for whom her dislike was growing. But it didn't work like that. Again, the thief's logic. She wanted to give that poor woman who needed a blouse to go with her slacks a hug. Feeling close to her gave Eve a rather desperate urge to *know* her. Of course she couldn't give her a hug, or even introduce herself, so instead, she walked quietly over to the rack from which she had taken the blouse, which was still in her hand, and stood beside her purse on the floor.

It was that feeling at the top of a roller coaster, the moment before the descent of the biggest drop. She crested the rise, then swooped down and lifted the purse off the floor. She slung the long handles over her shoulder and walked slowly away. She even paused, one department over, to inspect a chartreuse jacket. This wasn't theater, she wasn't trying to look nonchalant and innocent, she was truly interested in the jacket, which was a nearly luminescent green, a color that floated off the fabric. Eve could have taken *that* instead, but she wasn't supposed to shoplift from the department store. So she continued on forward, trying to remember exactly where her car was parked. Once she rounded the escalator, she stopped to stuff the purse into her own big shoulder bag, as any woman might do after making a purchase, and kept walking. She remembered that she had come in through Men's Apparel, so that's where she exited. Once outside the department store doors, Eve turned her face toward the bright yellow sun and smiled, eyes slit to protect her corneas, and let the warmth shoot straight into her pores.

The purse in her bag was a like a piñata. Or a box of Cracker Jacks. A blind date. A letter from Audrey. The contents were anyone's guess, but they might be richly rewarding. Eve sat in the front seat of her car, the vast parking lot surrounding her, the sun pouring in the window, and pulled the purse out of her shoulder bag. She let it sit in her lap for a moment. A supple, dark brown leather—to go with the wool slacks, of course—the kind that feels creamy to the touch. A simple zipper closed the one cavity and Eve pulled it slowly, like she was undressing Audrey. That thought made her pause, laugh. Yes, unzipping Audrey. The tiny *zzzzz* sound was lovely and satisfying. She reached her hand in before she let her eyes enter, remembering Halloween parties where peeled grapes were eyeballs and wet noodles were brains. Instead she felt a small packet of paper. Letters? A leather rectangle. The wallet probably, and it was fat. Loose coins, a pen, a tin of mints. She was about to open her eyes, going first to the letters, or what she supposed to be letters, when a shadow crossed her car. Two hairy hands clamped on the open sill of her window. The torso of a headless man, but not voiceless, for he said, "Ma'am, would you please step out of the car?"

"Sure." Eve tossed the purse in the passenger seat.

The detective's back was to the sun, and she was facing it, so she saw only a black cutout of a man. She imagined he looked like most department store detectives, including pocked skin, too much hair product, and a blocky body. She smiled at the sun, again, well aware that he would think she was smiling at him. Also well aware that, although she was forty-three, she wore a purple miniskirt and a sleeveless top, cut low enough to show the swell of her small breasts. That guy didn't know that she was a former Olympic runner. He didn't know that she was a national expert on grace. But he probably knew that she looked good.

Even Audrey had given her that. Cockles and mussels alive, alive-o. She claimed, not with words, oh, no, she wouldn't stoop to even talk about it, but with her entire being, she claimed to be unimpressed with the words "Olympic" and "best-selling." What interested Audrey was the pretty waif girl with her shellfish cart. A poetic image. Hawking whatever she had. As if grace were just desperation turned inside out.

"What do you need?" Eve asked the detective, and asked it seductively, not because she wanted to get away with something, because even though she knew she looked good, she knew that looking good at her age can annoy men. No, she spoke to him seductively because she *wanted* to annoy him. Make him want to say, "Oh, don't think that'll work with *me*, sweetheart."

He asked to search her car, so she said, "Sure," as she reached in her bag for her cell phone. In her peripheral vision, she saw him lurch, and she smiled, realizing that he thought she might be reaching for a gun. Right, she thought, just call me Louise. Or was that Thelma who blew the guy away? But her moment's amusement passed quickly when, looking at the dial pad of her cell phone, Eve realized that there was no one, no one at all, that she could call.

An hour later, at the station, Eve closed her eyes as another man took both of her wrists in his one big hand. She looked for and found pleasure in the dry warmth of his skin. She concentrated on the softness of the pads on his fingertips and at the base of his palm, the way the bird bones in her own hands rested against these pillows of flesh. She even looked for the pleasure in the cold hard metal encircling each wrist now, the ache of its chill on her tender skin. A ratchety clank and the cuffs had her hands in the perfect position, behind her back, for the beginning of her yoga routine. She could bend now, reaching her connected wrists up behind herself, as she leaned forward, gravity flipping her hair over her head, her hamstrings stretching. But of course she didn't bend now. She searched for the next possible bit of pleasure, like looking for the next stone in the crossing of a swift cold creek. The best she could do, and this would be a slippery stone, was the face of the booking officer.

Not unpleasant. Not ruddy red or unnecessarily hard. In fact, he was a large, pudgy man, with fat cheeks, a broad nose, and overgrown eyebrows. A moment ago, before he'd cuffed her wrists together behind her back, she might have been able to run. While still looking up into his pleasant face, she laughed at the thought of herself in flight with a law enforcement officer in pursuit, and this, it turned out, was what he didn't appreciate.

"Lady, there ain't nothing funny about what's happening to you."

Just then another officer entered the booking room with a print-out in his hand. He said, "Two priors."

"Huh," the big guy grunted his approval. "Nothing even remotely funny."

"I laugh when I'm nervous," Eve tried to explain.

She shouldn't have said "nervous" out loud. The word disturbed the air. Concentric circles of what felt like an electric current rolled off of her. The booking officer jerked, as if he'd been shocked.

"Sorry," she said.

He put a hand on the place between her shoulder blades and gently pushed. Eve closed her eyes again, not wanting to see where she was going. When she opened them, just five steps later, she was in a cell. The booking officer stood in the doorway, looking at her. She guessed he had been waiting for her to open her eyes. He said, "Booking vestibule. Someone will come get you for security and medical."

Then he shut and locked the door.

Eve looked for the pleasure.

This could be a locker room, she thought. A locker room found in an archeological dig, which would explain the absence of steamy showers, wooden benches, handy lockers, and of course, human flesh. Unless this were an archeological site like Pompeii, in which case there might be a mummified woman, bent at the waist, standing where the showers had once been, her right arm stretched down to her ankle, her hand in the claw position. Would the archeologists have ever figured out that she had been shaving her legs when the volcano erupted? It was possible, after all, for a Pompeii to happen here and now. Mount Saint Helens blew, so Mount Hood could blow, too. And if it did, this was where she, Eve Glass, former Olympic athlete and best-selling motivational author, would be immortalized. In the holding vestibule at the Multnomah County Jail. This was not a locker room, after all.

The cinder block walls of the vestibule, which were no more than four feet wide and six feet long, were painted white, semigloss. Eve lowered herself onto the cement bench and stared at the white cinder blocks. If this place were a black hole, one of those light-swallowing pits in the universe, she might be able to escape. The light that she was would be sucked through to the next universe. The beauty of black holes is that while no light can ever escape them, they are the birthplaces of stars. The end and the beginning all in one. But this place here, this holding vestibule, was a white hole, not a black hole, a place so brightly devoid of stimuli that all the energy coming from oneself ricocheted wildly off the walls, gathered, filled the room. No worm holes to the next universe. This room was like a blank slate, with nothing to absorb the energy, so there was only Eve looking at Eve. Maybe if she considered that shiny white cinder block wall a screen onto which she could project herself, she could watch herself like a movie. Stopping the random way her energy was glancing off the walls would help. These Multnomah County law enforcement officers thought their jail, their handcuffs, the words "two priors," were the primary terror for prisoners, and perhaps to some they were, but the classic bare light bulb would be what destroyed Eve.

Who she was now was not something she wanted to look at.

Sobriety

1/MY (FIRST?) BOTTOM

December 31, 1982

"Forty—and still meeting men
in bars whose stories—delivered
   in a wash of alcohol
and received that way—it was thought

   I should remember. Brilliant—
in the course of my bicycle
   toolings about town, coming
upon the greeting of faces

   I knew I knew with *my* high
five, the generic 'Hi, Guy!' There
   was a pattern: friends I thought
were mine were distancing themselves

   from me: Shelley B, who sent
a note disclaiming our friendship:
   no reason given; Harry
B, who read me the riot act

   on my 'condescending' bar
behavior. Well, to pass New Year's
   Eve, at least there was Roger
M. Nope! He would be rounding off

a dinner foursome I'd not
been asked to join. The night found me
    at Sporters gay bar downing
martinis in the company

    of Pat S, more fan than friend,
more tipsy collaborator
    than either." *You'd exhausted*
Boston—or it had you. New York

    promised a deepening of
intimacy with family
    and the lit crowd—and more sex
than you were managing to have

    here. Yet every effort made
to get you off (a drafted P
    and S away) availed you
nothing. JUST MAY HAVE SAVED YOUR LIFE.

2/JANUARY 1, 1983

"On what I thought was a whim
and not what it seemed thereafter,
   the last conveyance leaving
my station, I decided I

   wouldn't drink on New Year's Day,
curious to see if doing
   without booze would have any
effect on me. Did it ever!

   I went from being someone
whose walls and ceilings were coming
   down around him to angel
of the house—in one day getting

   my drawers in order. That night
found me at Skipper's, a ginger
   ale in my hands, mourning a
self who had lost the power not

   to spend every night of the
week in a bar—which I sensed I
   would now be able to claim."
Day three: you'd "forgotten how to

   walk" and "are losing your mind."
"No, back rub offered by my date
   for Symphony doesn't help.
A call to Billy M, a friend

   and alcoholic who was
likely to know what even non-
   alcoholics like myself
go through when they stop drinking. No

answer: break date; take myself
to meeting I brought John V to
    months ago." *Now there was your*
alkie, nightly knocking himself

    out with six-packs. JOHN, WHO MAY
HAVE NEEDED IT, NEVER RETURNED;
    YOU, WHO MUST HAVE FOUND SOMETHING
YOU WANTED FROM IT, GOT ON BOARD.

3/FIRST BOONDOGGLE

"Deciding that I *wouldn't*—
not that I *couldn't* in safety—
    drink, I declared myself a
member of the Arlington Street

    circle of love and was met
by resistance from one of its
    members. 'I'm having trouble
with the newcomer denial

    about their alcoholism':
thus spake John J, who seemed by
    articulateness to 'take
possession' of the meeting. 'You

    thought I was alluding to
you by my comments?!' he told me.
    'That's how self-centered you are!'
Ten years later I asked John if,

    having gotten off to a
bad start, we might now become friends.
    His reply: 'Maybe in the
next life.' The next life must not have

    looked far away—he was near
death by then, having believed, as
    he averred at meetings, that
'God hadn't gotten [him] sober

    to give [him] AIDS'—that is, that
codes of safer sex behavior
    didn't apply to him." *The
circles of love have proved themselves*

often enough circles of
detestation—face it, haven't
   you stayed sober to spite John
J, who expected you to drink,

   not because you were convinced
you were an alcoholic? Now
   that John's gone . . . TALK ABOUT YOUR
CASE—YOUR *CASES*—OF DENIAL!

4/I CAN SEE CLEARLY NOW

"The purple foyer walls were
a mess of peelings, the result
    of my having painted them
years ago without a primer;

    the bathroom ceiling had a
hole in it big enough to drop
    a body through—my hiring
Rodney B for renovations

    was part of the same New Year's
resolutions that led me to
    stop drinking. By day nine, my
inner walls and ceiling had come

    down too—as approaching the
church basement blackboard, chalk in hand—
    I said to the group, 'I had
always thought myself a success,

    having transcended (the line
climbed off the board) the bourgeois needs
    of work and love. Now my life's
line seems to have started well, then

    plunged into the shitter.' Sad
parabola." *The last pieces
    of furniture you bought for
your Revere Street digs—a super*

    *refrigerator (you ate
out) and a tea table (never
    touched the stuff), what needs did they
answer to but for round-the-clock*

ice cubes and gallons of gin?
"Look at yourself": is this what he
   meant, the friend of Tommy S
at Sporters you turned down and who

   then took your inventory?"
YOU OBSERVED AND THERE YOU WERE, A
   MAN WITII A PIID. WHO'D
BECOME SOMEONE'S BOOZY DOORMAN.

5/SECOND BOONDOGGLE

If you admitted you were
an alcoholic in pursuit
of recovery, you had
to go to meetings for the rest

of your life, so that you could,
what? in hewing to "the Steps"
lose everything that made you
you? You knew of drunken poets—

did you know any who had
gotten sober? "That's where a trip
    I made, ninety days sober,
came in handy. At meetings in

    the Village, I heard poets,
novelists, actors speak about
    being sober and going
on with their art: I wouldn't have

    to sacrifice a self to
'the program' to have it work for
    me: what was left but for me
to surrender to *it,* which came

    about during a Broadway
theater production of *Cats,*
    in which Grizabella—and
wasn't I as bedraggled from

    years of head-banging about
the bushes as she?—is conveyed
    up into the Other Side
layer: she would get a new life,

    a fresh start. I wanted one
too, and through eyes veiled by tears—or
    with a mind focused by them—
I saw only one way for me

    to get it: to go back to
Boston and assert I had a
    disease." YOUR FINEST HOUR—AND
IN YOUR LIFE (THANK YOU, THANK YOU) MINE.

6/INTO THE LIGHT

for Paul Schmidt (1934–99)

> *When Paul Schmidt asked, the last time*
> *you saw him alive in Cambridge,*
> *   if he might sleep sometime in*
> *your new digs, you murmured "Maybe"—*

> *   after all he did for you!—*
> *snatching you—back from Paris in*
> *   '66 and eager to*
> *demonstrate competency, new*

> *   to you, in Greek—from out the*
> *Esplanade's caressing darks and*
> *   into light. Literary*
> *lights they were at a dinner at*

> *   which you feasted on Lamb, Charles*
> *Lamb's "Dissertation upon roast*
> *   pig" being, at one point, on*
> *the discussion menu, as what,*

> *   at others, was not—in Schmidt's*
> *townhouse, with a library! on*
> *   Dartmouth Street. Brightest among*
> *those gathered lights was Richard H,*

> *   whom you would be privileged*
> *to take for the next fifteen years*
> *   as your friend and mentor. "Yes,*
> *but I gave as well as I got!*

    In the copy he inscribed
to me of his own translation
    of Rimbaud, for having brought
him in '83, just three months

    sober myself, to his first
A.A. meeting and the first day
    of what would translate into
fifteen years of sobriety

    and numerous luminous
translations," PAUL CREDITS YOU WITH
    HAVING GOT HIM OUT OF (HIS)
OWN "SEASON IN HELL." *This is yours.*

7/ LOVERS AND A FRIEND

"Before Craig, Eddie, Maxim,
there was drink, a fifth of liqueur
    loosening my trousers the
first time I had sex with a man.

    How else did I envision
the career of teaching, to which
    I aspired, but as one long
faculty party over which

    martinis presided—a
vision Albee's 'Virginia Woolf'
    uncomfortably confirmed?
And liquor helped negotiate

    the claims of my college (frat)
and my early gay (bar) lives, those
    irreconcilables then.
Later, when the lovers, the jobs,

    and the possibilities
of moving out of (or even
    within) Boston seemed to have
vanished, the drink stood at my side."

    Suddenly, before you had
proved whether or not you could not
    drink, you cut it, on a whim,
out. Was that any way to treat

    a lover or *a friend? Time*
passed and then . . . a chance encounter
    in a restaurant, where you
asked for non-alcoholic beer

and drank half of it before
you realized—ah, that blessed
relief—that you were with your
old friend. And you put the bottle

down, proving, of course, that you
could have just one drink and put the
bottle down. YOU CAN ALSO
GO ONE MORE DAY *WITHOUT* A DRINK.

8/ADDING AN AFFILIATE

"I'd gone six months without a
drink and there I was, again, crammed
    into half of two closets,
one "confessional" opening

    into the other (or closed
off by it), recapping my 'sins'
    to a man I didn't know
who, from his vial of poppers,

    offered me hits, incense of
which I did not partake—unless
    being in such close quarters—
so pervasive was the stench of

    'Amy' in them—amounted
itself, in a program I was
    already working, to a
slip." *Reflect on how you spent your*

    first night free of alcohol,
on your knees, taking dictation
    in Combat Zone "offices"
that are all gone now, as "acting

    out" behavior on your part
was not, having anonymous
    sex being important to
retain as an option, you thought,

    now that drinking was not. you
only hadn't drunk too much in
    the dawning of your Love Quests
so as not to blunt your late night

    skills in giving pleasure and
receiving it. Another sort
    of soberness? Another
band of flagellants! But is it

    in your interest really
to have no way left of acting
    out? YOU'LL BE SURPRISED AT WHAT
CAN BE DONE WHEN YOU ASK FOR HELP.

9/TOO LITTLE, TOO MUCH

"An abusive father of
four; a married bisexual
    who wanted to cut the dyke
out of herself; Sis G, a dyke

    scared by her history of
S/M; and Saul S, whose 'bottom
    line' included not locking
eyes with anyone for longer

    than three seconds—regimen
of his which I sought at meetings
    to demolish with my hard
stares, so delightful a country

    did immersion in those dark
pools portend; Julio; Pauline;
    the two Mindys—'Fuck' or 'No
Fuck,' according to whether she

    was able to curse or not;
and I, married to convenience,
    not a man: what we trusted
the meetings and their aftermaths

    to supply us with was safe
passage, first, through Saturday night,
    by means of one vast dinner
spread on Beacon Hill and a film . . .

    and then through life." *What did Saul
of the Deflected Eyes later
    see in his mirror but a
pierced and tattooed San Francisco*

  bar back—and the cynosure
of all eyes! And Sis? She cried up
    a meeting for sexual
anorectics, so far had her

   pendulum gotten away
from her. YOU LITTLE KNOW WHERE THAT
    PENDULUM WILL TAKE YOU ONCE
YOU SET YOUR SIGHTS ON SWINGING FREE.

MICHAEL HYDE

Life Among
the Bulrushes

T HE ONE NAMED April is the first to go. Daniel Peale collects
the brown caterpillars that have slipped from their spidery
tents in the wild cherry trees and gives them names of people
he knows and doesn't particularly like—names belonging to
the smiling schoolmates of his ninth-grade class, names of distant
relations, names of TV stars. Standing over the small fire he's built on
the dry shore of the backyard pond, he plucks the plump caterpillars
one at a time from a Tupperware bowl. He lets the one named April
drop into the fire. Flames catch the tiny hairs on her back. April
shrinks and shrinks and disappears.

Before he drops each caterpillar, Daniel speaks its name aloud:
Patrick, Cousin Michael, Sandra Bullock, Barb, Jenny Jones. If any
of the caterpillars manage to escape—perhaps by a gust of wind or
bad aim that sends it far from the fire—Daniel will let those go. If
Mrs. Peale interrupts in the middle of this judgment as she often
does, Daniel will also let the caterpillars go. He's convinced moments
such as these, small and unexpected triumphs, are moments of truth,

67

intervention, and faith, designed elsewhere by powers he could only hope to challenge.

This time, the one named Patrick is blessed enough to miss the fire completely. Jenny Jones, however, isn't as fortunate but drags herself somehow from the flames. Daniel watches the two survivors crawl slowly off, moving away from the heat. He licks his fingers before killing the fire with dripping-wet handfuls of pond clay.

Inside the house, Mrs. Peale is preparing for the trip to Ocean City, shoving clean and dirty clothes into duffel bags. She's packed the Styrofoam cooler with grape soda pop and Budweiser. When Daniel comes into the living room, holding the empty Tupperware bowl, Mrs. Peale straightens and raises a cigarette to her mouth. "I told you about using my good plastic," she says. Daniel shrugs and tosses the bowl onto a pile of dirty clothes. He knows Mrs. Peale takes every opportunity to make him feel younger than he is. When she looks at him, he's sure she doesn't see a fourteen-year-old with long legs and big arms and promising thick black stubble. Instead, she sees only the boyish cowlick, his light unaging eyes, and the silver braces along his top row of teeth that Daniel blames her for not taking care of years ago, when others his age were going through the same thing. Only at nights is he free to become who he has wanted to become full-time. He'll reconsider wrestling practices, the head coach who also teaches physical science and suits up in the same locker row. A force like that of God has stood next to him, naked, revealed, a body made purely of moss on rocks. Daniel volunteers for a demonstration, the Fireman's Carry, his body up-ended and mouth stretched as his face meets the foam mat, a weight as if the whole world has violently seized him, only to whisper, warm-breathed and with sincerity, "Mine," into his ear.

"We're leaving in the early morning," Mrs. Peale tells him.

Daniel knows this, has known it for weeks. He won't be going with his foster parents, Mr. and Mrs. Peale, but will stay home to look after the grandmother. Referring to the Peales, Daniel doesn't use words like *Mother* and *Father* because these words sound wholesome to his ears and imply connection. He likes to imagine that his true parents—the one man and one woman who united and made him and whose last name is something other than Peale—are dead. They died possibly in a horrible collision/explosion soon after his birth. He's told himself this story so many times that he's come to believe it.

Daniel knows why he was brought here thirteen years ago to live with the Peales: Barb Peale is *barren*. No matter how hard Sam huffs and puffs, there's no hope for his wife. Some nights, the gypsy moths bump against the window screen, and Daniel pictures Sam and Barb, grunting and prostrate like animals, foolishly hoping for something to take hold and grow.

Daniel's on his way to the backyard shed to fetch beach chairs when he spies Grandma Peale sitting on the screened-in summer porch. "Urgugurh," she utters. Since her stroke eight years ago, Baba's been confined to a wheelchair and the whims of her son and daughter-in-law. Wherever they choose to leave her is where she remains. Most often she can be found in a corner of the porch overlooking the pond, staring at one point in the distance. Before the stroke, she'd been a real presence and, in Daniel's mind, the glowing ember in the dying light of the old house.

He remembers the time, in a religious fit, that Baba had gone about the house nailing crosses above every door and smearing raspberry preserves—convinced it was a form of ram's blood—alongside every jamb. He was only eight years old and how excited he was to hold the jar for her as she dipped into it again and again with the table knife! Small blobs of the preserves had oozed onto his hand, and he licked at them, holding the tart delicious flavor in his mouth as he followed her from room to room. He'd lie on the goose-down comforter at the foot of Baba's bed while she'd read silently from her black Bible. The light on the bedside table was just enough to keep the room from falling into that still uncertain darkness of night. Mouthing scripture silently to herself, Baba would touch her forefinger to her tongue before turning each page and only speak when she'd come across a particularly important passage. Then, her eyes would grow larger, an "Ah-ha" would slip from her, and Daniel, suddenly alert, moved closer, staring at her as words on a page transformed to truth. John 3:16. Matthew 7:1. Mark 16:16. *He that believeth and is baptized shall be saved; but he that believeth not shall be damned.* First Peter 1:7. *The trial of your faith, being much more precious than of gold that perisheth, though it be tried with fire, might be found unto praise and honour and glory at the appearing of Jesus Christ.* She made Daniel commit these verses to his head—over and over again like songs that lodge themselves in memory—and would reward him with pear candies or allow him to select a beautiful button from her sewing box. She warned Daniel not to fall into the same ignorance to which her son and daughter-in-law had so unfortunately committed themselves, a world of material things and present-day, a world entirely closed off to divine grace and guidance. Nights like this, a yellow brilliance waved from Baba's eyes. He almost feared her, for she gazed so intensely, as if she really could see that slight yet troublesome pillbug of disbelief scuttling about inside him. Before switching off the table lamp, she'd tug on Daniel's ear affectionately and make him recite her favorite: Matthew 9:22. *Daughter, be of good comfort, thy faith hath made thee whole.* Daniel's lips would still be poised in the circle of the final word when Baba would smile and fall back into her pillow, closing her eyes as if sleep had come that suddenly.

Sam and Barb have never thought officially to remove the crucifixes that Baba put above the doors—there's certainly too much effort involved in sliding a stepladder to each one. Some have loosened themselves naturally, however, and if made of glass or porcelain, have broken to pieces on the hard floor. For so long, Baba was convinced an angel was coming to carry her away. This was all before that day eight years ago when, staring into a cat's-eye marble she'd plucked from the decorative jar atop the refrigerator, Baba Peale closed her eyes, counted to ten, and had a stroke. Since then she's been unable to utter a word. Only short pieces of sound pass from her mouth. Though it's quite possible these sounds are a jumble of intelligence, no one can understand her. He's reluctant to believe that her talk about the bright light of God, about the passage from life to death to eternal life, has ceased. When he looks at her sometimes, at the thin gray hair clinging tenaciously to her pink scalp, Daniel catches glimpses of what Baba used to be peeking furtively from behind those eyes.

The backyard pond rests under a layer of mist. Mosquitoes and fat swamp flies skim the surface, lowering their heavy abdomens to the water and expelling eggs. The swamp water is green-gray and oily. A small rowboat that children might pole to the middle of the pond sits on the shore. Hidden amid beggarweed and arrowgrass, frogs twitter, calling to one another. It's a softer version of the voices that speak to Daniel during the night, reaching out like warm hands from the dark center of the pond. And now, the way Baba continues her unintelligible sounds makes it seem that she's calling back to them.

Daniel cannot get over Baba's patience. The time he'd crucified a dead bird, the time he'd lowered a banana spider into the ant farm, any time he'd tested the tenuous thread between life and death, Baba was the only one to look past his behavior. She believed his testing a good thing as long as he showed faith and fear of the Lord. Daniel knows that Barb and Sam have discussed often in soft voices whether they should return him to where he came from, to maybe let him try another foster home. In recent years though, Sam's started making excuses for Daniel's behavior. Sam says it's hormones. Barb says it's run-off from nearby Three Mile Island that's gotten into Daniel's skin and makes him act so, though she adds that he's always had way-above-average test scores. The existence of these, excelling in one area and failing miserably in another, confounds her.

Barb's calling from the other side of the house, yelling, always, as if her leg's caught in a clamp-trap. Daniel remembers the lawn chairs he's supposed to be finding in the garden shed and carries them to the front of the house. Barb drags a suitcase along the walk, with three duffel bags slung over her right arm. She chooses to appear as the martyr. "Help me load the car," she says.

"Why don't we wait until Sam gets home?"

"Because our vacation starts at 5:00 PM. For all of us, whether you're going or not."

"You're not going anywhere until tomorrow morning."

"Doesn't matter when we're going. It's a state of mind." Daniel knows Barb's fond of slipping things in like that, finding some way of tying the physical world to the mental at every opportunity. She thinks it makes her sound smart and modern.

It takes six more trips to and from the house to load the station wagon. Daniel carries the Coleman coolers, a bulging suitcase, the beach umbrella, a hot-air popcorn popper. When it seems they might be running out of room, Barb decides they should unload everything and try again. "There's got to be some way to make it work."

While Daniel unpacks and repacks the car, Barb leans under a red maple with a glass of lemonade. Daniel sees her look once at the whispering tents of caterpillars that have invaded the tree. She points, as if to object to their presence, but remains quiet.

Later Daniel thinks things have finally worked out until Barb comes from the house carrying three inflated beach balls. A sudden wind takes her by surprise and sends one of the balls blowing about the front yard. "Oh, no," Barb says, the way Daniel has heard her say it when finding a pot of water boiled over or a page in her trade paperback dog-eared.

Barb chases after the runaway ball, going, Daniel thinks, with the zeal of a child hunting Easter eggs. He thinks how unfortunate she looks: her thin brown hair flying into her face and open mouth as she runs. When she stops to retrieve the lost ball, the other two somehow escape her. Every time she goes running toward them, she kicks them by mistake. The harder she tries, the further they seem to go.

"Help me get these," she yells.

It doesn't take Daniel long to rescue the balls. But once he's done it, Barb discovers there's no more room for them in the car. "I spent all morning blowing them up," she says and looks as if she's going to cry.

"You need to let some air out."

"No. There's got to be a way." She pushes two of them through a side window where there's little space. The plastic moans. Daniel waits, expecting the balls to pop, but they don't. Barb stops to wipe sweat from her face, then puts her hands on her hips.

There's the sound of gravel, and when Daniel and Barb look, a car has pulled into the drive. A large woman gets out, carrying with her a leather case. She's wearing a thin dress patterned with brilliant orange and pink flowers—blossoms both opened and closed—that remind Daniel of morning glories the way they climb and seem to wrap themselves around the woman's body. A straw hat is balanced perfectly level on the woman's head. She's smiling too much, Daniel thinks. Her pale, round face is unblemished except for a circular scar by her mouth that stretches itself bigger the more the woman smiles.

"Hello, neighbors," the woman says.

"Oh, no," Barb's immediate reply. Daniel remembers then that Barb and this woman have had run-ins before.

"Pardon me?" the woman says.

"Can't you see we're ready to make a trip? Can't you see that?"

"I can see that very clearly, Ma'am. If you'd only give me a moment—"

Barb grips the beach ball in one hand, meaning to do damage. "We don't need any Witnesses," she says. "You can take your brain-washing somewhere else."

"If you could give me one moment to tell you about—"

"No, thank you." Barb starts toward the house, still holding the beach ball.

"Perhaps the young man here thinks differently. He's old enough to make choices for himself." The woman's noticed Daniel staring at her. He's not so much interested in what she has to say as he is in her being on the front lawn. He takes it as a sign.

Barb grabs Daniel by the shirt. "Come inside. These people don't know when to quit."

"You're doing a great disservice to that young man by forcing deaf ears upon him."

"I'll take a pair of those deaf ears for myself," Barb yells back, slamming the front door.

The fat woman does not move from the front yard. She stands firm and immobile, like the lighthouse she believes she is. "Go away," Barb yells from behind the living room curtain. "We don't want you around here. Get out of my yard or I'll call the police."

Daniel and Barb watch the woman approach the house. She's come down the walk, up the front steps. She rings the doorbell. Daniel admires her persistence.

"I'm warning you," Barb yells.

The fat woman rings the bell again and again. It has become, in a way, a game.

Barb goes into the kitchen and comes back with a golf putter of Sam's. She opens the front door and waves the golf club like a flag.

"I warned you. We're not interested."

"Well," says the woman. "The Lord led me here for a reason. I can only go so far."

"You can go on in your car. What's the name of your person in charge anyway? That's who I'm gonna call. What's his name?"

"You should know him as God," the woman says. She crams the leather portfolio deep into the crook of her arm and does an about-face, walking down the drive.

Barb doesn't go away from the front window until she's sure the woman has gone, and then flops down on the living room sofa that lets out a sigh of dust. She stares at the ceiling fan whirring overhead. It wobbles and is missing one of the propellers. Daniel thinks the whole thing could fall at any moment.

Barb takes a deep breath and lets her hand droop over the edge of the couch. "Why don't you go get me an ice water?"

WHEN IT'S that time of day for her to be indoors, Baba lets her head roll to the side like a weak-necked doll and leaves a trail of drool spilling from her mouth. Daniel pushes her to the living room, into the corner beside the clock where the comings and goings of her wheelchair have managed to keep a square of floor free of dust.

Sam gets home from work at the post office where he's postmaster and changes into Bermuda trunks and a T-shirt. He looks not like a postmaster but like a college professor, with his gray beard and shiny head. He opens a can of beer and raises it in a toast. "To vacation," he says. He smiles at Daniel, like they're brothers. When Sam speaks to Daniel in private, sometimes sitting on the edge of Daniel's bed and smelling of drink, Sam likes to use the words *respect, trust, faith,* and *honesty* in talking about his relationship to Daniel. Daniel usually waits for Sam to kiss him good-night before rolling over to face the wall.

Now that Baba's in her corner, the Peales and Daniel have dinner at the Sinking Springs Family Restaurant. The walls are decorated with charcoal drawings of wild game. A stuffed deer greets patrons at the door.

"You wouldn't believe how much misdirected mail there is," Sam says, poking his knife at the air. "Today I counted fifty. And you would think it's because people move on, their mail gets lost, but the truth is people just aren't careful enough."

"Have another roll," Barb tells Daniel, pushing the small wicker breadbasket at him.

"You have to be careful with addresses. A simple mistake, just forgetting one number, one small thing, can mess up the whole system."

The waitress, whose name is Debbi, asks if they need anything else.

"We're going on a trip," Sam informs her. Daniel dislikes Sam's habit of telling complete strangers about his business.

"Oh, I wish I could go on a trip. I bet this young fella is gonna have himself a summer romance." Debbi pats Daniel on the shoulder and when he smiles at her and says, "I'm not going," she draws back.

"It should be a wonderful trip," Barb's saying. "Ocean City is such a magical place. We're meeting my sister and her kids there. We go there every year."

Daniel can remember all the thirteen summers he's lived with the Peales as one because there's been little variation. They stay at a place called Misty Harbor that's at least ten minutes' walk from the beach. They each lie unprotected in the sun until their skins turn red so they can complain about sunburn for the rest of the trip. They get their pictures taken as a group by gamy camera boys who roam the beach flattering girls and making small talk with the adults but who don't think to look at him and smile. Barb Peale always agrees to the photographs, but when the time comes, they never go to pick up the photos and pay. That makes at least thirteen photographs of the Peales: lost, probably destroyed, never to be seen again.

IT'S AS IF the black earth has risen up and surrounded the house. There is no moon and the night is cold and nothing seems to exist beyond the window screen except for the sound. Daniel hears Barb and Sam leave when the clock reads 4:00 AM. It's a six-hour drive through boring Pennsylvania countryside and cramped New Jersey, and Barb and Sam want to get to Ocean City in time to spend the entire day at the beach. Daniel hears the departing station wagon, imagines the red brake lights flickering at the end of the driveway before the car turns onto the road.

He sits up. Even in the dark, his feet find the floor.

Grandma Peale lies at the center of her bed, curled like a fetus, and murmurs from troubled sleep. Now Daniel realizes how very small she is, how much she has diminished over the years. He slides one arm beneath her neck, the other under her legs, and lifts. She's a bundle of sticks. Her eyes open. "Don't worry," Daniel says. Baba starts to mutter, slow and sleepily. Daniel remembers how she used to speak of black nights such as this as a time when the spirit of the Lord would possess the house and watch over every one of them. She'd tell the story as if the spirit were a wave and a flood with no hope of escaping its goodness.

Maneuvering Baba through her bedroom door is easy, down the carpeted stairs that let no sound escape, onto the porch. She doesn't struggle. Outside, Baba in his arms, Daniel doesn't bother to lock the door. He hears it slam shut behind him. That's enough.

He looks at the pond and sees it in a new way. Once the pond was declared DEAD by the State. For that year it was a HEALTH HAZARD and was glossed over with a slick, impenetrable sheen. Fish floated stiffly to the surface, and for days there was the noisy cackle of wayward seagulls picking at the dead. Then the birds were gone. Then not even a single crayfish scuttled between rocks. The year after, however, things cleared; if you looked hard, you could see new life: waterboatmen, gadfly nymphs, snails sliding over the black muck still clinging to the bulrushes. And now—not long from sunrise—voices of frogs and even spring-peepers have settled. Daniel feels conviction at this renewal of life and the revisiting of sounds to the pond. There is this new life pulled from death.

He lowers Baba into the rowboat and pushes it from the shore. He doesn't mind if he gets wet. Baba's sleeping again, peacefully now. He poles the boat toward the center of the pond. There have never been oars as long as he can remember. Only a long, unwieldy pole to push into the mud and move the boat slowly around the pond. The rowboat's movements make patches of thick algae pulse like hearts.

Daniel has read the story of Moses, thinks it, in a way, the most important story of his own life. This is one reason he feels that he and Baba are one: they are both abandoned, like infant Moses cast among the reeds. And in that story, Moses was found, and saved; he grew and prospered. Until Moses let himself be seized by faith and belief, he doubted God's intentions, questioned Him. With the appearance of the burning bush, however, God's love and Moses's love of that love were soon indisputable, inescapable.

Daniel looks at Baba sleeping. It's possible she knows what's going on. Daniel likes this idea that she knows, that he's not alone in knowing.

In spring there would be a slight current here, running just beneath the surface toward the end of the pond away from the house where there's a small stream, a rivulet Sam calls it, that only flows when the water is high. The heat's lowered the level considerably, and here, the deepest point, is only ten feet.

The Peales will be gone for eight days. They will not check in with him for at least four. He has made sure of this. It has to do with that thing *trust* he and Sam have discussed. Sam says that he *trusts* Daniel as long as Daniel promises to call in an emergency and have no parties. Daniel promised, and this made Sam smile and admit he was so happy.

Daniel's given himself these four days to be touched by a higher power, to discover there's more to his life's plan than serving as foster son to Sam and Barb Peale. Surely God will show himself and complete the ring of Daniel's faith, filling in that one still questioning piece just as He did for Moses. Daniel's made rules for himself which include staying in the boat and doing without food or water. The same is true for Baba. Moses was provided for, and Daniel expects similar provisions. If for some reason the boat comes into contact with shore, he will pole it to the center of the pond again. He knows he will recognize God's presence when he sees it. It can come in many forms, he supposes, though he must be careful to keep to these rules he has set for himself. If this hasn't happened within the four days— the time limit he's given himself—he knows what must happen— and additionally what *has* happened—to him and Baba.

Looking at the house sitting like a blister on the dry yellow grass, Daniel squats in the boat and thinks: Yes, I will test God.

B Y AFTERNOON, Daniel has rolled all of his clothing into a tight ball and wedged it into the prow of the boat. He is entertained by the appeal of his own body, the jut of his hip bones. The sun is unrelenting. He's undressed Baba to that point just before indecency. A white bra clings to her shriveled breasts. Her underwear reveals a slight circular stain, now dry. Daniel looks at her skin, at the thick blue veins pushing dangerously close to the surface. A scar in the shape of a frown—from a gall bladder operation long ago—stretches just below Baba's navel. It looks raw, as if it's never healed properly, though Daniel knows this can't be true. He's about to touch it, but draws his hand back, sticking his fingers into his mouth, touching them instead with his tongue.

Since getting into the rowboat, Baba has been quiet. He watches her stomach rise and fall. The scar stays a frown, moving between *more* and *less* severe.

Only once does the boat drift in any direction, and even before the temptation of shore can be a threat, Daniel poles back to center. Baba lies on her side. Her lips move and she sometimes blows bubbles.

Already he can feel the sun tightening and reddening his skin. He looks at the water all around him. Even though the deeper parts blend into numerous shades of blue and onward to black, he thinks it must be warm, from being caught in such a small warm place. He won't touch it. Not even when he feels thirsty does he move toward water. He tries to sleep in order to avoid the heat.

A ROUND EVENING, around the time Daniel thinks it must be evening, he watches the red circle on the horizon. He stares at it, as if waiting on a clock, wanting it to move faster, to fast-forward time.

Male dragonflies slide against one another, jockeying for territory, crossing like swords. He sees at the edge of the pond, near a cluster of cattails, small black shapes that slip silently into the water and disappear. They could be muskrats, diving terns, something he does not know. He keeps expecting one of them to surface by the boat. He looks down into the water, sees nothing but his own face, and watches the sun again.

IT'S NIGHT. Baba tries to move. Daniel sees her tiny body reach toward water, but he pulls her back. He's much stronger than she is. When he looks into her eyes, saying, "No, Baba, this is for us," he sees a tear and rubs it away with his thumb.

Even though the night is cooler, his skin's still warm from the day. He doesn't need a shirt, though he dresses Baba again. He watches her finger trace the wood patterns along the side of the boat.

When his stomach growls it reminds him of all the frogs, now emerging from daytime hiding to chirp and disrupt the night and keep him company. The moon this night is only a piece of the whole. But still it makes the pond look like it's lit with a swimming pool's submerged light. His head's so weary he thinks for a moment the light's coming from inside the earth.

TWICE DURING THE NIGHT Daniel wakes to the sound of wings. Twice his eyes open expecting angels. Twice he closes them to sleep again.

THE SECOND DAY Daniel begins to think that maybe Sam and Barb, for some reason, are on their way home. Perhaps one of them's forgotten something. Perhaps they've heard voices in their sleep and decided something is wrong.

Daniel thinks that it's an important thing to be loved, and if the Peales, Sam and Barb, do in fact love him and Baba, they will come. He imagines love works that way: it's an invisible wire between people so the slightest tug can be felt miles away.

When Baba starts crying, he kisses her on the forehead, and says, "I love you."

THERE IS A slightness to Daniel's head. The smallest movement, the most insignificant sound captures his attention all through the second night. Gurgles and pops begin just beneath Baba's chest. Her face has turned bright red from the sun, though he's tried to protect her with his own body, his own shirt.

This night he tells her about three wonderful orphans who wound up not so alone because of their faith and persistence. During the story of Orphan Annie, Daniel thinks he sees Baba laugh. "Yes, that is a funny one," he says. "A very funny one. Imagine: a man named Punjab."

He's still laughing when he realizes that she's asleep.

H E TAKES TO PRAYING. He feels tired and his head is light and the skin covering him is bright pink and parched and ready to flake.

He thinks now how it is, this thin flimsy line between life and death, this line that divides yet unites. His understanding began years before when he smashed a housefly in his hand and took the time to look closely at its lifeless body. One moment the fly was moving, the next it was reduced to a small wet jumble of parts. When the spirit dies, the body dies, yet if the body dies first, the spirit surely lives on.

Daniel sits, twirling the pole in his hands. Baba doesn't move much anymore. He lays the pole across the boat and slides his hand to the naked flesh of her stomach. He pats her there, meaning *everything will be okay.* He finds himself caressing the jagged scar just under her navel. He traces the arcing path with his fingertips and changes direction when he has come to one end.

H E DOESN'T KNOW whether it's night or day. Light has become something he's forgotten, though he's watching a group of ducks chase each other around the edge of the swamp. He half sees them, for they soon lose their shape and become colors.

"Baba," he says. "Look." He turns her head so her eyes face that direction. Her head rolls effortlessly back into place. He's thinking about the next day, tomorrow, when it'll be time to enter the water, to feel its desired coolness finally wash over him. His test of God will be complete, and he will not be the one who's failed.

Now Daniel notices for the first time the woman floating down the small sloping yard to the shore. She stands with her hand raised to the level of her eyes. She looks large from the center of the pond and is wearing a hat and a brightly colored dress. "Hello," the woman calls out. Her voice sounds muffled, much further away and unreal. She starts waving her thick arms. He cannot be sure, but Daniel thinks he can make out flowers—orange, pink, and fuchsia flowers— their large petals curving and reaching one over the other toward sunlight, or is it toward the heat rising from the water's gray surface?

"Young man," the woman calls.

She glimmers and fades, glimmers again.

"Young man."

Daniel feels words crawl to his lips, towing themselves through him, up and down and through him, until there's no part left untouched. His head barely propped on the edge of the boat, he smells the yellow decay lifting from the water. "Here," Daniel calls. This time louder, "We're here."

First Fist

Never enough of orange or the rest of light.
Rest your head on my mortal shoulder,
time stretched between us sheer as a cat.
In the coil of hair and its mystery I lay my head.
Anyway, the clock doesn't know your name
or the date of your death. Birth me again
in the wounds of your sweater. Sweeter
the second time and those thereafter.

After

After you die, I will fly to France in August.
I will stand in a field of sunflowers
body caressed by petals, like the hands
of all the men who've touched you gathered
to hold me through this grief. Then, the flowers
will collapse, fold their leaves like arms buried
across your chest. Their yellow will drain 'til
their heads are black stones leashed to the earth
by their broken stems, their failing bodies.
Oil will drip, waiting to be used,
like my blood, lost with no where to rush
without you. Lover, I will follow
our flowers to the ground, soil my fingers
with dirt from the only place that was just ours.

JEFF OAKS

Mistakes with Strangers

I pulled down a man's pants in public once.
I had said I love you earlier and I had meant it.
Don't ask me why. Two men later I was him,
betrayed. I pulled off the next man's wings
in return and I found out he went on to own
and run a large company that manufactured
a kind of shoe that was so beautiful you had to buy them
but so heavy it was impossible to lift. Some people died.
Help me, Rhonda, Jesus is not coming for me.
I stopped returning his calls. His wounds
made a boring centerpiece for conversation.
He kept asking me to stick my finger in them
all the time. The next man stuck me
with a three-hundred dollar sexline phone bill
and vanished. I liked his thick body that was like
an ice cream cone I could not lick away.
Later, I was told he was a professional
ice cream cone, whatever flavor you wanted,
at the corner of 6th and Wood downtown.
So I paid. One man I stuck with a three
year depression—well, he said—that required
a therapist, two women chiropractors, three new jobs,
and four other lovers before it lifted. Later,
he thanked me for being so cool. One man
I left handcuffed to a bed, since he was always nicer
unsatisfied. Once I tried an orgy but found myself
thinking in the middle of it all, this: we're a pack
of lions clawing, eating, roaring over the body
of a crippled zebra, which is also us. Then I fell in love
with the least pushy of the bunch and acted as if
he alone meant anything. We fell off the bed
to be alone. I saw him again only twice more,

since it required an eight-hour drive and I was poor. After
the second time, he decided he had to write a poem
right then and I put my clothes back on and sat
on his screened-in porch. Crickets, katydids, big
furry brown moths came to cling on the screens.
I examined their armored, hairy undersides with
cocktail toothpicks while his typewriter clattered.
What was the meaning of such machinery?
Cats howled and screamed. The poem went on for hours,
it seemed, and turned out only to be a letter
to his mother, who he said was crazy. I apologized
and took the next bus home. The next week
I was paying for a therapist, looking for
a personal trainer I wouldn't fall in love with.
That was a mistake too, since it meant I had only
myself to impress and that trick never works.
Once I slept with a man right after his wife died.
He said it was her last wish. Once a man promised
to make me a star. Once a man drove his brand new car
directly toward a tree to see if I'd flinch or scream,
which is how he recognized care. I said
I'd welcome death and groped his crotch. He
turned away. I had late night dates with another man
who turned out to look so much like my father
when he was twenty five—in a photo I never saw—
thank God—until years later. I'd meet him
in his shower at precisely ten o'clock.
For a while I pretended to be the plumber
who needed to check out his pipes. After
that wore off, we'd usually end up sitting together
on the shower floor while hot water rained down. We'd
sit there and admire our feet getting cleaner
and cleaner near the drain. Usually he'd be drunk
before I even got there, and want to talk about
his first lover's suicide. When I wouldn't agree
to tie him up and then punch him until he fell asleep,

well, that was that. He yelled faggot at me
from a car once when I was walking on the street.
Once I slept with a man who was kind but
not attractive at all, just to see if I could make
what I thought was the right choice. Forget
running with scissors or dropping pennies off
the Empire State Building or swimming right after lunch.
There was only had to have, have, had, had it with.
One man I nearly killed myself over I ended up
laughing about. Another I laughed at then now I miss
like the best goddamned dog I ever knew, who
I could tell anything to, who listened even though
he could never help me which did help in the end.
I was ordering drinks on a plane to Europe
when he got put down. Sometimes I still
feel his big warm weight beside me in the night
and turn toward it before I think, oh, right.

CHARLES JENSEN

Metrosexuality

I, too, dislike it—where have cowboys gone,
their sandpaper denim so rigid with cotton pulp
it chafes the curled hair from their legs?

Or the suggestive divot of button-down shirts
where a boutonniere of chest growth
bursts from among the seams and closures?

Every strip of city land developed into skyscrapers,
curbs, one-way streets. All that was left
was men, their shuttered landscapes

rough: a deep peat marsh in the armpits
where thick-stalked reeds emerge
from oil-thick waters.

The eyebrows with their shadowed eyebrow
in between. Weathered faces that witnessed
decades, salt-and-pepper hair.

Where do we put the men
not that we have manicured their borders?
Where do we stack their bodies,

cold plastic kindling for a blue-smoke fire.
And who will preserve their dirty, imperfect fingernails
even as another arm burns under their razor?

ROBIN BECKER

Salon

Acolyte at the font, my mother
bends before the basin and hose
where Jackie soaps her fine head,
adjusting pressure and temperature.
How many times has she
bared her throat, her clavicle,
beside the other old women?
How many times the regular
cleansing and surrender to the cold chair,
the sink, the detergents, the lights,
the slick of water down the nape?
Turbaned and ready,
she forgoes the tray of sliced bagels
and donuts, a small, private dignity.

Vivienne, the manicurist, dispels despair,
takes my mother's old hands into her swift
hands and soaks them in a bath to soften
the cuticles before the rounding and shaping.
As they talk my mother attends
to the lifelong business of revealing
and withholding, careful to frame each story
while Vivienne lacquers each nail
and then inspects each slender finger,
rubbing my mother's hands
with the fragrant, thin lotion,
each summarizing her week, each
condemning that which must be condemned,
each celebrating the manicure and the tip,
the good half-hour spent at Vivienne's station.

Sometimes in pain, sometimes broken
with grief in the parking lot,
my mother keeps her Friday appointment
time protected now by ritual and tradition.

The fine cotton of Michael's white shirt
brushes against her cheek as they stare
into the mirror at one another.
Ennobled by his gaze, she accepts
her diminishment, she who knows herself
his favorite. In their cryptic language
they confide and converse, his hands busy
in her hair, her hands quiet in her lap.
Barrel-chested, Italian, a lover of opera,
he husbands his money and his lover, Ethan;
only with him may she discuss my lover and me,
and in this way intimacy takes the shape
of the afternoon she passes in the salon,
in the domain of perfect affection.

JAMES CIHLAR

Blue Heaven

Driving back to work after Goodwilling
on University Avenue, Saint

Paul, during my lunch hour.
There goes Ryan the Plumber.

Shear Pleasure. Salon
of Beauty. Christian music

played at the Salvation Army.
I held up a thick china plate

from the fifties, blue and gray
border, atomic shapes,

Blue Heaven. Phil's Oriental
Foods. Servicios en Espanol.

Where is there a public toilet
in Frogtown? Frogtown toilet?

Stetson China began in Chicago
in 1935 and operated until 1965,

Ebay said. Bill won't like this, but I found
a stack of Colonial Interiors for seven bucks

at the Saint Vincent de Paul.
He doesn't like clutter, and moans

when I bring more into the house.
How do you handle the difference?

Sally will ask a week from now.
I pretend every comment is a joke.

How funny. Every single one.
Twelve piece feast. Drive Thru.

Behind the farmers' market,
next to El Amor,

a vast empty parking lot,
abandoned strip mall,

Desnick Bros. Drugstore, white reversed out of purple.
I must have that sign.

These people, Saleema knew, were content to assess and disregard her casually as a big, strange, black spot in their daily commute. And she had learned, as she grew out of the parameters of normalcy, to keep things to herself. They did not need to know that this spot could gaze, could read their disquieted faces, and be completely in love.

MECCA JAMILAH SULLIVAN

Powder and Smoke

EYES CLOSED, she fell through the doorway carelessly, blissfully, and landed on the bed as though there were no doubt in her mind that it was there and ready to catch her. She cupped her hands over her breasts and smiled inside herself as she smelled that girl's cigarette smoke in her braids, around her eyes, on her skin. Lying atop piles of clothes on her quaking dormitory bed, Saleema was full and content, and she made plans to live her life in that girl's smoke, with or without her. This feeling, high and unconquerable like some unnamed constellation, made her thank God for the dizzy mornings that came after she prayed to be taken in her sleep.

The blue-and-white flicker of the small TV above her head lit the tiny room sporadically, discovering in flashes Saleema's piles: mail from home, mail from school, bills to pay (these wedged in the crevice between the bed and the garbage can), old issues of *Essence* and *The Writer,* Lane Bryant and 16 Plus shopping bags, empty salt-free cracker boxes and sugarless grape juice cartons. But she did not see any of this. In the new smoke that entered and filled the space with her fall, Saleema was only aware of the few things in the room that could feed the urgent joy that girl had inspired in her. In her shoulders she felt the colorful letters from her homegirls that she had pinned to her corkboard, remembered the Jay-Z and Biggie poster on her closet door, the dead flowers, still in the vase, sent from her only real admirer.

She even noticed the muffled bleat of the television in the room next door, and through the bliss of smoke she detected a man's voice and the words "Sealy Posturepedic, Serta Perfect Sleeper, and Simmons Beautyrest . . . even lower than the leading quality flatbeds."

"Dial one–eight hundred–M-A-T-T-R-E-S," She belted without regard for key or tune, "And leave off the last *s* for Savings!"

SHE LAUGHED out loud what was in her chest and sang the song again with the soul of Aretha and the deliberate style of Ella. Then she sat up. The little room was a mess, and with a smug grin in the mirror, she confirmed for herself that she didn't care. But she moved some things around anyway to give movement to her hands and legs, and to make space for the smoke and her happiness. The colorfully collaged shoebox she used to hold her blue and purple and orange nail polish was spilling out of the narrow foot space in her desk, and the splintering chair careened against the refrigerator door. She squatted, careful not to knock anything over with her head or behind, nudged the box under the bed, and pushed the chair in at the desk. Then she stood up and looked around.

"WE HAVEN'T seen you, Saleema."

"Yeah, girlie, where ya been?" The chorale of white girls at her doorway chirped the inquiries with pink-faced smiles.

"It's like every time I knock on your door you're not here."

Saleema parted her lips and shrugged blankly through them as she stepped shoeless into the hallway and shuffled toward the vending machine. A Diet Coke and a thirty-five-cent bag of Linden's Butter Crunch cookies, like from the bodega at home.

"Hi, Saleema." A smile and a wave as she pattered down the steps.

"What's up, Saleema? I tried to call you." This one had passed out drunk on Saleema's floor a week earlier and had not spoken since.

"Hey, Saleema, how are you?"

Saleema acknowledged these greetings as vaguely as they came and grabbed her navy pea coat from its hook in the dormitory foyer. She slid the soda into one pocket and the Butter Crunch into the other, looked down at her socked feet, and left the building. Outside the ground sent cold through the thin white socks, and a sweeping afternoon shadow made the ivy-and-brick college look like a cardboard city, built by cold hands and disowned by the sun. But when she stepped off of the last front step, that sun filtered through her lashes and hit her cheeks with the soft sting she had always loved to write about. She smiled at the air and when she saw the Northbound Blue-Line bus across the street, she got on.

THE PEOPLE on the bus watched as she struggled through the narrow door and up the three steep steps.

"Free ride." The driver was a stone-faced Latina woman, and Saleema imagined that her smile, when elicited, must be wide.

A little white boy with pencils in his hands grinned as she maneuvered her body through the shiny silver poles. He wondered why she was so big.

The guy with the pink hair in the handicapped seat looked at her shoeless feet and nodded.

The dreadlocked Black woman smiled because Saleema reminded her of her daughter, and the beautiful white lady with the thick eyebrows and silver hair scowled and turned toward the window.

These people, Saleema knew, were content to assess and disregard her casually as a big, strange, black spot in their daily commute. And she had learned, as she grew out of the parameters of normalcy, to keep things to herself. They did not need to know that this spot could gaze, could read their disquieted faces, and be completely in love anyway.

At the dormitory, the white girls wondered where Saleema had gone so abruptly on a Saturday afternoon. And without any shoes on, at that.

SALEEMA PUT HER bare feet up on the seat in front of her and began to sing a medley of Janet Jackson songs quietly for herself and anyone who cared to hear her. She rested her head on the window and waited for something in the glass to call her out of her corner seat.

Lost in the rapturous glide of "When I Think of You," Saleema had not noticed the small man who rose and was now walking toward her. His shoelaces were untied and he wore a dried powder-blue carnation on his lapel. His eyes were clear and glazed like glass marbles, and his cheeks and brow shone as though he were about to greet an old friend. As he approached, Saleema noted that the man smelled faintly of rotten oranges, and when he extended his hand, she hesitated a minute before taking it.

"Can't wait, eh?" He thudded into the seat in front of her and Saleema moved her feet.

She raised her eyebrows and nodded slowly, loving this man's strange appearance.

The man rubbed his face and tapped the pole as he spoke. "It's like I always said—better to just wait and see. Always hard though, y'know?"

Saleema looked open-eyed at the man and waited for more.

He had paused and was gazing at the cough syrup advertisement overhead. He jerked suddenly and faced Saleema with imploring eyes.

"I'll never leave again. Now say what they want, these crazies will, but I'd rather stay where I know, now that I know. That last push outta mama's tum-tum, you watch. Every baby, the president and his shit cleaner, they cry cause they wanna get back in. I say stay where y'know, or find it where y'go, if y'can." He shook his head slowly as though in pain and closed his eyes.

The lovely mean white lady was now standing clasped to the last silver pole. She caught Saleema in an accidental glance that was disconcerting at first, then comforting in its comedy; the woman had known immediately that this big, barefoot black girl was a shame. And now look at the company she was keeping. By the time the white lady had slunk down the steps and the fluff of feathers from her unseasonable winter coat had floated all the way to the bus floor, Saleema's strange companion was asleep.

The white girls at the dormitory said they hoped Saleema hadn't been nabbed by lunatics, but in truth, they weren't so convinced of her humanity as to afford her vulnerability in their imaginations.

Saleema sang "Escapade" more quietly so as not to disturb the sleeper.

THE SMOKE was still stuck in her braids and so she took this time to take in its glory and remember that girl's opal skin and galactic eyes and smile, the hips that curved like a bud vase and sprouted into the arms that wound like stems and the hands that were fine and tight like tulips. Saleema closed and smiled in again.

When the driver called Sovereign Street, Saleema noticed that this was the first time the woman had spoken since she got on. The sleeping man rose abruptly and flew off the bus in one motion, and without so much as a glance in Saleema's direction. A quiet disappointment trickled in her chest as she watched his back in flight. This man had engaged her in his bizarre conversation, fallen asleep on her, and then left unexpectedly without so much as a strange or silent good-bye. And though it dismayed her a little that this man had so effortlessly reached her interior, Saleema had to fasten her coat and press the dirty yellow tape by the back door. The driver raised her eyebrows in the wide rearview mirror and opened the door again.

The ground on Sovereign Street was colder than at school, and the soda in her pocket chilled her thigh now that she was fully vertical. She looked for the man but found only a nickel on the ground. This was probably better, she decided, as it was almost definitely unwise to follow eccentric white men around unknown streets. And good luck was just as exciting as the man had promised to be. Saleema picked up the penny and smiled at the sight of her feet. She crossed Sovereign Street and entered the Sovereign Street Comic Shop, where she purchased a five-cent piece of Bazooka Joe bubble gum. Under the store's small awning she unfolded the little paper that accompanied the hard powdery nugget. *Bazooka Joe is playing baseball, and his friend accuses him of stealing third base. Impossible, says Joe. My pockets aren't big enough.* Saleema flipped the paper over to read joke #357: *What did one elevator say to the other? I think I'm com-*

ing down with something. This was disappointing. Saleema popped her gum and looked around.

Across the street a little boy with cornrows wrote curse words on the ground in blue chalk, and back at the dormitory Saleema's disappearance was no longer a topic of conversation; midterms and Saturday evening affairs were at hand.

COOLNESS AND the setting sun made Sovereign Street a hard, gray place, so Saleema had begun to look for a heated spot to warm her feet. She was feeling around a narrow street for such a place when she saw her sleeping man on the stoop of an abandoned building. She stopped at a mailbox and fiddled with it long enough to see the man stand slowly and sail further down the block with a smooth, important stride. She walked a few yards behind him, realizing that love and curiosity were overwhelming the limitations of her sensibility, and when the man entered the huge teal-colored building on the corner and held the door open behind him, Saleema followed right in.

The gaping room did not even smell like oranges. Saleema was disappointed by Bazooka Joe's punch lines and confused by the path the small man had spun for her, but she still felt the ardor of that girl's smoke in her shoulders, and so she went along with it all. It did not surprise her that they all looked like him, bore his same height and weight, same attire with slight variations. She loved the perfect congruence of their precisely pinned carnations (this one lavender, that one paisley, this one aquamarine), the contrast of the room's absurdly high ceiling and the low-reaching heads of its inhabitants, the old gray walls, somehow vibrant and tangled with their deep-voiced banter. Most compelling, though, was the fact that they were all working diligently at small blue machines. They were Dorothy's munchkins, Alice's playing cards, and now Saleema was not surprised at all.

Standing at the room's entrance, Saleema noticed that the walls were lined with large bails filled almost to the brim with mounds of what looked like flour but smelled like the sweet fragrant powder that she had loved to love at home. Powder poured from the tubular end of each little blue machine into small cylindrical vats on the floor, and men with black-and-white speckled carnations drove tall carts up and down the aisles collecting the vats, filling the carts with powder, and leaving a thin white fog behind them as they went. Saleema remembered home as she remembered that fog, the sandwich bags full of white powder that she carried around Harlem for eight months of her fourteenth year (St. Valentine's till Columbus Day) concealed in the hole in her coat. She remembered fingering the wondrous texture every chance she got, rolling it softly between her fingertips, clenching it tight and full in her fists and then releasing it slowly through the tender cracks between her fingers, smiling in as she did now that the smoke was on her.

The playground on 152nd street and Amsterdam Avenue was always dark indigo in her memory, and it always smelled like platanos and chocolate thai with slow breeze and fast lights. The dented metal slides that burned bare legs in the summer and the broken tire swing remembered like home, and the powder was part of that. She remembered questioning the gravelly cement benches that prickled thighs and the chess tables that joined them, wondering who thought Black people would play chess in the playground when there was each other and home to engage.

THE COCO HELADO man and the hot dog lady should marry when we are jumping double-dutch my mama your mama sitting on the fence and loving powder because it is so soft and so texture turned into an adjective the texturest superlative and she was the only one who knew what it meant but she was not the only one who knew what it was at home playing house in the jungle gym and wondering why there was room for a jungle down the street from the stoop where every day was a block party in mood blue and little girls would steal your my little pony to bring on your first fight at home in the playground still loving that powder and being the only one when you leave and go to a smart people school a white people school and talk like you do and look like you do and can still teddy bear teddy bear turn around teddy bear

teddy bear touch the ground . . . saleema will remember celie and net-
tie's song and see it in herself and her girls will see the movie and
remember saleema's notebook and her powder and wonder where
saleema is now.

Saleema is inside of white powder where she was born and where
she lived under the lights that who knows how they come up early in the
winter and late in the summer in the corners by the fence where the red
ants were and you couldn't step on them but one boy would eat them
and you wanted to eat them too so that that one girl with smoke later
would giggle as you giggle she giggled saleema did when the old man
pissed on the basketball court after the church women had gone home
to do someone's hair and did you want some food and where is your
mother working hard, lord jesus, hardheaddedness was enough to urge
her into pussy and smoke and love and home like powder and everyone
knew her powder and her were deep and close like home because that's
what it was and home knew that throw yo shit / throw yo shit, saleema
when five-o comes they wont care bout the difference between powder
and snow, blow, yeya yo ass is crazy but they aint home don't know you
love you like the playground like smoke girl throw yo shit we smokin
weed and you got powder in your pocket girl don't you know you could
get us killed like eeney meeney miney mo catch us they will catch us and
we won't be able to holler . . . yo powder can get us killed.

F RANTICALLY, SALEEMA held her braids to her nose and sniffed
for the smoke in the rain in front of the building. She pulled
them, tugged them and twisted them, wrung them around themselves and inhaled desperately but she could not reclaim it and
there was no powder outside. She wanted to dance to her heartbeat
and conjure up the smoke that had left her hair in the powder
place, but the beat was too fast and her feet were too heavy to carry
her. She wanted to fall on her bed and feel home in her heart and
on her skin but her heart was flying away from her and her skin was
too wet to feel.

THE DORMITORY WAS dank and the white girls were preparing for a party.

"What's up, Saleema?"

"Where did you go?"

"No shoes today, huh, Saleema? Hehe!"

Saleema sat on the front steps and held her head as they shuffled in and out of the rain. She stayed that way until the moon was like platinum against an ink-black sky, and then she moved inside.

She should have grown used to making these realizations at her most naked times; she had made this one years before and sporadically since (over tops of silky heads in subway cars, in small, unyielding chairs, in photographs, and in front of bedroom mirrors). This time she was sitting on the toilet in a narrow stall when she presented herself with the fact: she was not a woman. She was too big and too black and too full of something thicker and deeper than blood to be a person at all.

She took the soda and the cookies from her coat pocket and placed them beside her on the bathroom floor. At the sink she was confronted momentarily with the beautiful black eyes that cried smoke and powder for the world, the lips that sang home in mattress commercials, and the cheeks that loved and smiled in. She focused on her hands and washed them thoroughly, wishing for lather to make powder and water to make smoke so that she could look at those eyes and sing home to them. She stood there for five minutes or so with that wish, heart bouncing like a little girl ready to leap into a twirling clothesline for double-dutch. Then she dried her hands on a paper towel and moved to the telephone in the foyer. She dialed her campus voice mail and listened to Biggie behind her on the outgoing message.

"What up, yall, this is Saleema. Leave a message. Peace." Her voice was thick and steady like syrup, she thought, a lie. She entered her PIN and waited for her One New Message to play.

"Now, bitch, you know we was just bumpin Biggie in the room so now you wanna throw some mufuckin Big Poppa on your voicemail?

Anyway, where you at? I'm just chillin, wondering what's going on with you—haven't seen you since like this morning. Anyway, I'm bout to smoke me a cigarette. Holla back. Love you girl. One."

Saleema's ears and feet were warm; she closed her eyes, smiled, and breathed deep.

Music

The husband leading us
to the water

even the black we wore was bright
moving across blond grass

afternoon unseasonable, warm
darkness already present

but also the feel of spring
in weeks the first daffodils

that first summer after swimming
she would send me upstairs—

There are clean towels, darling

his hand at the window latch
and she is lying there

one leg then the other perpendicular
her face telling

the pain, unbearable
as if such bodily insistence must be answered

with relief
at the broken latch his hand

his mouth set
against telling the private

So much of what I did was to please her

and when the moment comes
the gesture is abrupt, ceremonial

at the edge of the black water
his great arm bending

elbow rising in gray air
he holds the wooden box

he digs for ash as if for food
(the hunger was sadness)

And then, arm lifting, his hand
opened to the sky

and what she had burned to
rose, taking the light.

JOAN LARKIN

Amy Lowell's Erotic Audacity

A CONVERSATION WITH HONOR MOORE

HONOR MOORE is the author of *The White Blackbird: A Life of the Painter Margarett Sargent by Her Granddaughter* and of three volumes of poems: *Memoir, Darling,* and *Red Shoes.* Moore's essay on Amy Lowell and her choices of Lowell's work for *Amy Lowell: Selected Poems,* published by the Library of America's American Poets Project, reveal the powerful directness of Lowell's voice, notably in audacious erotic lyrics addressed to Lowell's lover and life companion, Ada Dwyer Russell.

Lowell published her first poem in 1910 at age thirty-six. Before her death at fifty-one, she published ten books of poems, a volume of Chinese translations, three books of literary essays, and a two-volume biography of Keats. She brought the work of the imagists to America, editing several anthologies of their work; wrote and spoke as an advocate for "the new poetry"; and toured the country with Ada, performing her poems to packed audiences.

JL: For most of us, Amy Lowell's name brings to mind just one poem, "Patterns"—and the famous last line: "Christ! What are patterns for?"

HM: Her using "Christ!" was a scandal—

JL: It's an eloquent antiwar poem and a passionately erotic one, but the scarcity of other Lowell poems in anthologies supports the assumption that she somehow deserves her sullied reputation. Pound's mocking epithet, "Amygism," has done real damage. What got you interested in Lowell's poetry despite the way it's been denigrated?

HM: I had read just one poem—period: "Venus Transiens," in Louise Bernikow's feminist anthology *The World Split Open.* I knew only that Lowell smoked cigars and was fat and was a lesbian, and I'd seen one photograph of her in some overwrought Boston drawing room. When Geoffrey O'Brien of the Library of America asked me if I wanted to edit a selected Amy Lowell, I said, "I'll read her and see." Having written *The White Blackbird,* I knew that world of wealthy, cultivated Bostonians and thought it would be fun to go back there—Margarett was born in 1892 and Amy in 1874. I was curious. I read Louis Untermeyer's *The Complete Poetical Works of Amy Lowell*—it was 550 double-columned pages of poems, and the print was so small that I had to get them Xeroxed and enlarged. I endlessly read them and read them, and I was intrigued. But when I started writing the essay, her work really opened up—that thing that happens when you learn more about someone's life. I was incredibly moved by the story of how she'd done all this preparation and study to teach herself to write—and how, on the brink of publishing her first book, she met this woman who was the love of her life, and how that completely broke open her writing. And there was something very moving about this rotund woman—Lowell was 5'1" and very fat. She had a glandular disorder, so there was nothing she could do about it, and it was humiliating to her. She was a passionate person who had the luck to meet someone and have it change her life. Then her love poems became as moving as they were good.

JL: I'd heard that she was a lesbian but still vaguely confused her with the heterosexual speaker in "Patterns." Was Ada her first lesbian lover?

HM: I don't know if there was carnal knowledge before Ada, but there was *something*. There were a couple of love poems in the first book. She didn't meet Ada until it was about to be published and didn't add any erotic poem to it after they met.

JL: What was the impact of that meeting on Lowell's work? What was the relationship between her erotic life and the lyric poems she wrote?

HM: Well, there's her poem "The Weather-Cock Points South." When it was published in *Vanity Fair* in 1919, it was titled "The Weather-*Vane* Points South" [*laughs*]. It's such a shockingly homo-erotic, lesbian poem—you can't believe that this cunt poem you're reading was published in 1919 by a lesbian whose brother was the president of Harvard! Then, you learn there was a particular woman who inspired it . . . ! Some of the poems are even more touching, like "Madonna of the Evening Flowers," which combines the erotic and the domestic in a way that's really beautiful. It's a moving portrait of a relationship—and a kind of *ideal* portrait of a relationship.

JL: How long were Amy and Ada together?

HM: They were together for thirteen years, until Amy died at fifty-one—she was young when she died.

JL: When I read *Baby Precious Always Shines,* Kay Turner's collection of Gertrude Stein's and Alice Toklas' love notes, it struck me that *all* of Stein's writing was in a way addressed to Alice. Alice was her lover, her spouse, her support, and her ideal audience. Do you see anything like that in Lowell's relationship with Ada?

HM: I think it's different because of the way Lowell became a poet. First, she became a reader of poetry: she quit her inadequate, proper girls' school at sixteen and finished her education by reading, first in her father's library, then in the Boston Atheneum. She fell in love with Leigh Hunt and Keats and Shakespeare—she really *discovered* reading. Of course, she wrote things that precocious children write, and her mother put together a little book of her things, but she didn't become a poet until she saw the Italian actress Eleonora Duse perform in 1902 and was so ignited she sat up all night writing a poem. It's as if she'd seen her muse—as Reneé Vivien wrote, "A woman appeared to me." She teamed up with her friend Elizabeth Ward, and they read and wrote together for eight years, teaching themselves to write poems. Amy was in love with "poesy"—like Keats, like the romantic poets; the idea of poetry was redemption for her. And when she met Ada—whose father had been a bookseller, so Ada was a reader—they could really talk. Ada knew about literature, and she had been in the theater; she had become famous, acting in the company of Eleanor Robson—who, incidentally, left the stage to marry August Belmont and become an important suffragette—a donor and feminist activist. So Ada was someone Amy could talk to about writing, but even before Ada, Amy was committed to poetry. And although her stronger poems are to Ada, she wrote lots of other kinds of poems, too: historical prose poems, New England narratives—I love the one called "The Doll," which is something out of the world of Sarah Orne Jewett, whom Amy knew, and certainly not something Gertrude Stein would have written. In Lowell's erotic poems, Ada is definitely the muse, but she didn't make use of a consciousness of relationship as an aesthetic context in the way Stein did.

JL: Many of the poems you chose are the erotic lyrics. Do you think that's her best work?

HM: Yes.

JL: What do you find especially striking about her craft?

HM: She has enormous nerve. She's not afraid to declare her vulnerability. A poem like "A Decade" is just so direct—almost flat-footedly direct—but the directness of feeling is what makes it work as a poem. And the language—for instance, the line "When you came, you were like red wine and honey"—it's not that "red wine and honey" is necessarily such an original image, but there's something so original about her using it that directly. It's not dressed up in any way, it's just—there.

JL: This kind of plain, direct speaking isn't fashionable these days. It's not what the critics love—though why should critics be the ones to tell us what poetry *should* be anyway? It's suspect to be that direct and vulnerable.

HM: Yes—and it was especially so in that early modernist moment.

JL: But I think that in a way we're still suffering from the inheritance of that moment. Now anything that's as full of feeling as her poems are is thought of as sentimental.

HM: But it's *not* sentimental. I'll read you "A Decade":

> When you came, you were like red wine and honey.
> And the taste of you burnt my mouth with its sweetness.
> Now you are like morning bread,
> Smooth and pleasant.
> I hardly taste you at all for I know your savour,
> But I am completely nourished.

The red wine and honey don't stand for anything other than red wine and honey. Her images often aren't metaphors—

JL: They're just the way things look and how they taste.

HM: And then there's "The Bungler":

You glow in my heart
Like the flames of uncounted candles.
But when I go to warm my hands,
My clumsiness overturns the light,
And then I stumble
Against the tables and chairs.

There's just such self-revelation there, of this awkward person—and of course we're all awkward in those kinds of situations.

JL: But we rarely write about it.

HM: And she's not afraid of being passionate. In "The Taxi"—again, it's that kind of direct, plain speech, and then it goes into a kind of crescendo with:

Why should I leave you,
To wound myself upon the sharp edges of the night?

I never did get around to asking the various Bostonians whom I know what they thought they were reading, when they were reading these poems!

JL: But her poems were very popular and celebrated.

HM: She sold very well, but my sense is that the poems she would perform all over the country were the more public poems and that the erotic poems we've been talking about were not the ones that she would wildly perform.

JL: What were the performances like?

HM: I think they must have been quite self-consciously formal and theatrical. She toured the country with Ada—Ada, of course, having been an actress, would coach her on her performing—and she'd travel with her own light to put on the lectern, and I think sometimes she had

dancers, and she had a man friend dress up as Napoleon for a historical piece in Josephine's voice. The readings were jammed—there were
people lined up, and you couldn't get in. They were performances!

JL: Of Amy reading poetry.

HM: And the other thing she did was to be an advocate—there
would be debates about "the new poetry"—there was a famous one
at the Poetry Society of America. She and Ada would get to a city and
check into their hotel suite—she didn't bring her dogs (she had
seven sheepdogs), but—it was a big event. And meanwhile, she was
ill—the last eight years of her life, she suffered. After tearing her
umbilical muscle while trying to pull their horse carriage out of a
ditch, she had eight surgeries, none of which cured her.

JL: Can you put her work in the context of her friendships with
Pound and the other imagists?

HM: She became acquainted with imagism in about 1913, which was
when H. D. was first published in *Poetry*, and immediately traveled
to London to meet Pound. She soon met H. D. and Richard Ald-
ington and D. H. Lawrence, whom she included in her imagist
anthologies; she also met Thomas Hardy and Henry James. At first
Pound liked her, but when she became a player, he turned against
her. I think most women poets slip out of the canon, but I think Amy
Lowell was drummed out! Some (particularly male) critics I've
spoken to say it was her own fault. Part of the problem was her club-
woman affect—that's what she knew; she had the sense of entitle-
ment of her position in Boston society, and she brought all that to
bear on the cause of "the new poetry." But what I say to those critics
is that if a man had done that, he wouldn't have been punished that
way. It was really because she was a woman, and because she was a
powerful woman. And probably also because she was a lesbian.

JL: They resented her class, her affect, her being a popularizer, her
power—

HM: Her power. And it kind of irritated them, too, I think, that she was also talented.

JL: It's easy to feel superior to someone who's having a popular success.

HM: Meanwhile, she brought imagism to this country. She edited three anthologies, published in 1915, 1916, and 1917, and she meticulously sent royalties to all the poets. But that's not what you hear about her. You hear that she was sort of this nightmare, officious dyke—you know [*laughs*]—and of course that's what *I* had heard, and that's what I expected to encounter. And I didn't.

JL: I half believed the mistaken notion that her poems weren't really very good, that her language was kind of cloying and overdone, and that she was the most minor of that whole group.

HM: It's not true! In fact, I think that her short imagist poems are stronger and more engaging than H. D.'s short Imagist poems—H. D.'s great poems are the long epic poems. Lowell's short lyrics are sensual and full. You really feel a presence.

JL: You hear a distinctive voice. Something I love about her is that she's not taking a High Art stance—it's not as if the poems are saying, "This is Literature." The poems are coming directly out of feeling, and the idiom is American.

HM: And these women—and men, too, for that matter—who were raised in those repressive, suffocating, ritualized upper-class societies, who were passionate people—I talked about this in terms of Margarett Sargent in *The White Blackbird*—they had to put it somewhere. Amy Lowell had a need to express that part of existence. And what's so powerful is that she was able to *do* it—in a full way—even though she had only thirteen years of a career.

JL: The misrepresentation and erasure Lowell's work suffered has happened to women artists again and again—the sort of thing Louise

Bernikow writes about in *The World Split Open.* The way Lowell
became an object of scorn is like what has happened to the confessional poets; the term has become pejorative, even though there's
some great poetry there.

HM: You keep thinking, Oh, God, do we have to read about this
again? Lowell says it in "Dissonance":

> I alone am out of keeping:
> An angry red gash
> Proclaiming the restlessness
> Of an incongruous century.

You always get this sense of her feeling that there's something wrong
with her—that she doesn't fit.

JL: How does her work hold up? Does she still speak to us?

HM: She speaks to *me!* I included the canonized poems, like "Lilacs"
and "Patterns," but the vast majority of the poems I included were
poems that I hadn't known and came to love. Donna Masini tells me
that she remembers Audre Lorde—who was Donna's teacher at
Hunter—talking about Amy Lowell as having been a great influence
on her.

JL: Yes, I can hear Amy Lowell in Audre. Their sentence rhythms
sound similar. And they both have the strategy of using strong
imagery, setting the scene and evoking a place in a sensuous and
visual way, and then this voice comes breaking directly through and
asks a question or makes a statement.

HM: That comes right out of Lowell's experience. It's having grown
up so solitary, I think, in the garden of her father's house, an extraor-
dinary garden where she spent so much time as a child. She was a
change-of-life baby, and so she's ten or eleven years younger than the
next sibling up. Her mother had Bright's disease and was an invalid,
and her father was very busy, so Amy was by herself.

JL: So it was like being an only child.

HM: And she was very open to the sensual world. Her experience was of being in a trance of sensuality all the time, and the voices would come out of that. Two poems in this book, "The Painted Ceiling" and "Climbing," are from a sequence of poems for children. They're ballad-y, very different from the rest—but you get the sense of this creature who lives through the visual and the tactile and the sensual—and in silence, really, except when the sensual world coheres and enables speech.

There's a sense in all the poetry of the presence of flowers and plants and bees, and I think part of what makes these poems powerful, and why you can tolerate all the flowers and moonlight and hummingbirds, is that it's *real* moonlight and *real* hummingbirds. In "The Weather-Cock Points South," there's that great image of looking through lilac branches at the stars, and you just know that it's something that she's *seen*. She has that in common with Keats: when he's talking about nature, you're there—and *he* was there. It's a kind of relationship to the vegetable world that's very rare now—that reality just doesn't exist in that way anymore. Because we've mastered it. But I don't think they had.

JL: It's not as usual for someone to grow up with a huge, lush garden—

HM: And there were more lush gardens then. It was more likely for someone becoming a writer then to have a relationship to nature; it was that vivid. Here's that line: "The stars crowd through the lilac leaves to look at you"—you can imagine looking through lilac leaves to look at the stars.

JL: And you can hear her voice speaking clearly and directly about the experience.

HM: It's a very unembarrassed, unapologetic voice. That's a gift, in a way, of her class situation and only-child-ness and knowing that your brother was the president of Harvard and your father's cousin was James Russell Lowell and your other brother was a writer and world traveler. You know, it's that world—

JL: Where you can speak and expect to be heard, and you have the confidence—

HM: Yes.

JL: Do you identify with that at all?

HM: Not exactly that, no. Amy was a princess. There was so much money for that generation—it was before income tax, and it was the servants and the great house—it was a whole kind of aristocratic life. Her assertiveness actually displeased the other women in her family. She wasn't supposed to do what she did as a woman, yet she was entitled by her position. Carolyn Heilbrun, in *Writing a Woman's Life,* talks about women artists who become significant first having to get widowed or have a marriage break up.

JL: They had to pay their dues and do the conventional thing before they could do what they wanted to.

HM: And Lowell was really let off the hook by her body—she had this heartbreak over a broken engagement, and then she tried to lose weight—the Dr. Atkins of the day, Dr. Willard Banting, advocated a diet of nothing but asparagus and tomatoes, which broke Amy's health and didn't work. After all that, she was free. So it's a combination of her money and position, of her being the princess, the adored baby sister of powerful big brothers, and the not-beautiful woman—and finding an outlet for all that passion.

JL: She was a lot luckier than Alice James, wasn't she?

HM: Yes.

JL: The alternative is horrific, when you think of it—

HM: And Charlotte Perkins Gilman—

JL: Robert Frost is supposed to have said, in the 1950s, "Someone ought to unbury Amy." It's a gift to us all that you've done it.

AMY LOWELL

The Taxi

When I go away from you
The world beats dead
Like a slackened drum.
I call out for you against the jutted stars
And shout into the ridges of the wind.
Streets coming fast,
One after the other,
Wedge you away from me,
And the lamps of the city prick my eyes
So that I can no longer see your face.
Why should I leave you,
To wound myself upon the sharp edges of the night?

AMY LOWELL

The Weather-Cock Points South

I put your leaves aside,
One by one:
The stiff, broad outer leaves;
The smaller ones,
Pleasant to touch, veined with purple;
The glazed inner leaves.

One by one,
I parted you from your leaves,
Until you stood up like a white flower
Swaying slightly in the evening wind.

White flower,
Flower of wax, of jade, of unstreaked agate;
Flower with surfaces of ice,
With shadows faintly crimson.
Where in all the garden is there such a flower?
The stars crowd through the lilac leaves
To look at you.
The low moon brightens you with silver.

The bud is more than the calyx.
There is nothing to equal a white bud,
Of no colour, and of all,
Burnished by moonlight,
Thrust upon by a softly-swinging wind.

GREGG SHAPIRO

Still Talking

Watch his mouth, the way it anticipates
silence. It is a mouth conversant with
the history of oral sex in the men's rooms
of Greyhound bus stations. The misshapen
teeth, an offensive color, could tear you

another ear, another ulcer. Why does he
bother to shave? Nothing could possibly
cover that orifice, not sheet metal, redwood
bark, wax paper or steel wool stitching.
If he's told you something once, a borrowed

joke or a moral in an authoritative public-speaking
tone of voice, you will probably hear it again
and again, without the slightest embellishment
or pretense of truth. The jokes aren't remotely
funny, though he struggles to tell them without

bursting into uncontrollable giggles, and
the morals are immoral. The sloppy kisses
he sends over the phone to voice-mail victims
are the sound of skin being pulled from a bone,
one layer at a time. Rent boys line up to

relieve themselves into that quivering oval.
He throws his voice effortlessly, when you
least expect it, and the ventriloquists are
so jealous they refuse to speak without
moving their glossed lips. In photographs,

his mouth looks like a cartoon drawing
of a mouth, a courtroom artist's rendering.
Even when he whispers, his north-side-of-Chicago
accent cancels appetites as far south as East
Peoria. Once, a dentist tried to cut out his

tongue while he was under anesthesia. Never
had the dentist seen anything like it; a tongue
with treads like a steel-belted radial tire.
He still talks when he coughs, heaving words
that sound like "cough, cough, choke, cough,

gag." Please don't ask me to describe what
it sounds like when he eats. I only have
the stomach to tell you about his speaking
voice. The way it sounds when it insults
and condescends, especially when he thinks

he is being complimentary and cajoling.
The way his voice rises to the pitch of
a popular high school cheerleader's squeal
when he laughs. He has a chin, which wasn't
there the last time I looked, but I remember

seeing it once, jaundiced and greasy with his
saliva. Watch the corners of his mouth, the way
they betray his interest in what you have to say.
Notice the way they are poised for interruption,
how they barely tolerate dialogue.

Portfolio

TEE A. CORINNE

ZIPPERED METAPHORS

I HAVE BEEN fascinated by erotic imagery since the early 1960s, earlier if you count my stepfather's *Playboy* magazine centerfolds. Pictures with lesbians as subject matter were hard to come by, but I treasured those I found in reproductions of work by Rubens, Toulouse-Lautrec, and Boucher. Primarily in the 1970s and 1980s, I created my own explicit and evocative sexual pictures. Although I have exhibited portraits, landscapes, and still lifes, my erotica has been seen almost exclusively in lesbian-themed publications.

In the imagery for which I am best known (the "Sinister Wisdom Poster," "Yantras," "Intimacies"), I have created "solarized" negatives, a process that has been around since the 1920s and can be seen in work by Man Ray, Lettice Ramsey, and Winifred Casson. Solarization is a dark-room manipulation characterized by strong outlining and partial reversals from positive to negative. I like the surreal, otherworldly quality that it gives to photographs.

Unlike some of my other artwork, the "Zippered Metaphors" series has appealed to men as well as women. Perhaps this is because the images are sexual, but not gender-specific. For this series, I arrange unattached zippers, usually in pairs, thinking of them as bodies interacting with one another. I became interested in zippers when using them as subjects for drawing in classes I teach. I was taken by the many meanings that individuals brought to the idea of "zipper." For me, they offer intriguing formal problems, cognitive resonance, and imaginative opportunities.

TEE A. CORINNE

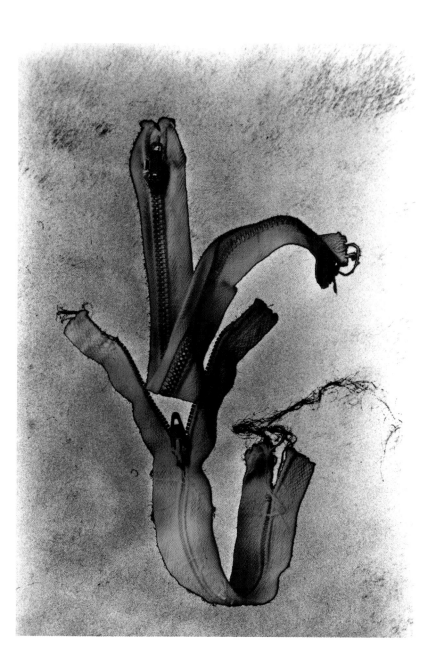

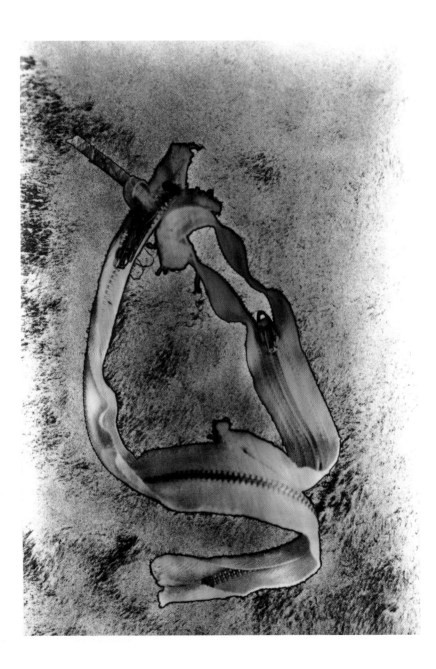

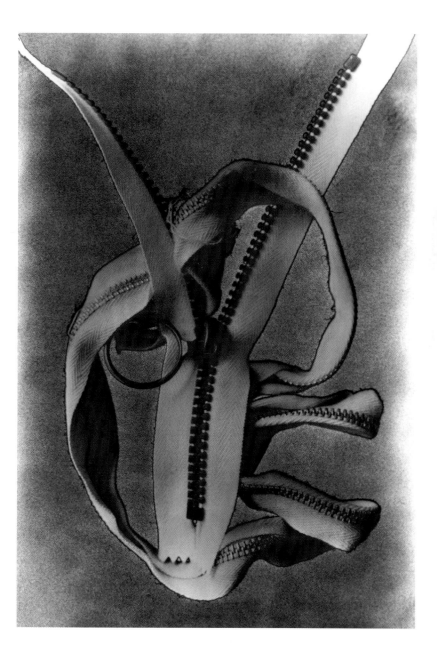

AT ABOUT the time this issue of *Bloom* goes to press, I will be moving to a new live/work loft for the first time since 1987. The move has brought about a consideration of personal history and how it's reflected by objects and images.

As I look around my space and think about what to pack and what to discard, it really comes down to the notion of *collection*. How many things have I collected in the last 18 years? Or in my 49 years of living? Specifically, as an artist who has made photographs since high school, my place is filled with pictures: on the walls, in flat files, magazine cutouts in folders, framed images wrapped in bubble wrap, gifts from friends, snapshots of lovers, a box of old family photos inherited from my grandmother, and on and on.

Instead of simply publishing new photographs in *Bloom* (which was my first inclination), the five images I've submitted are a sequence from the last 40 years. The earliest chronologically is the picture of the boys running. This was actually taken by my older brother at summer camp in the early '60s, but it is printed from a negative I have printed numerous times since discovering it in the late '70s. The two photographs of the wreaths were taken in 1990 as friends and acquaintances were dying of AIDS. The wreaths were part of a Veterans Day memorial in New York and left up past their prime. The wilted flowers were a potent image that spoke to me of the deep loss I was feeling at the time (and continue to feel to this day). The blue image of the plaster cast was shot at a Victorian-era museum in the small town in Connecticut where I grew up. Though I made the photograph recently, I visited this museum frequently when I was young and the place provided my first exposure to both "art" and also images of naked men. Town legend has it that when the museum opened in the early 20th century, the locals were so offended by the male genitalia that the museum had to be closed so the genitalia could be lopped off and replaced by plaster fig leaves.

These four photographs, along with that of the red couch, are a tiny fraction of the thousands I have in my house. To me they speak of the beauty and complexity of the world while suggesting that images, like stars and humans, are impossible to count, burn bright for the briefest moment, and then, casualties of history, cease to exist.

BILL JACOBSON

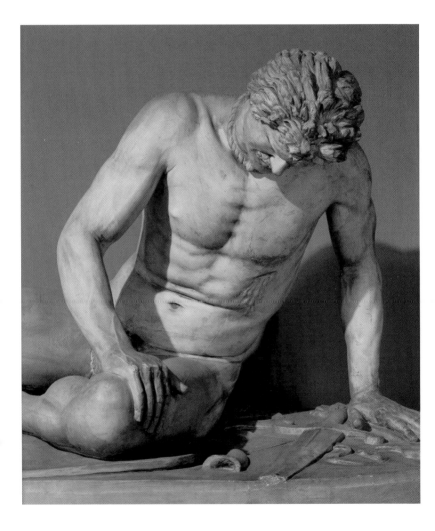

Portfolio
JOAN COX

FLOWER PAINTINGS/
VENICE PAINTINGS

M Y CURRENT body of work is inspired by individually wrapped bouquets of flowers seen at open air markets. The wrapping forces the flowers into random organic patterns that fill my canvases. The flowers themselves are expressionistic splashes of color with intimate linear details scratched through the layers of paint. I also spent quite a few canvases recently interpreting scenes of Venice—capturing the color of the water and the rich history of Italy. Most of these pieces have pages of Italian literature and some printed photos of piazzas as the underlying structure of the painting.

JOAN COX

PEGGY SHINNER

The Knife

I N MY MARTIAL ARTS TRAINING I'm learning to use the knife. *The* is the operative word here: *the* knife. The definite article, underscoring the definitive nature of the thing itself. That's how we talk in my dojo: *the knife, the bo, the jo, the sai.* All the weapons made preeminent by language: no indefinite *a* for any of them. But the knife, well, the knife is in a category of its own. *Bo* and *jo*—the long and short stick, respectively—and *sai*—a three-pronged, trident-like instrument—have their origins in agriculture; at least that's one version of martial arts history. Originally tools used by Okinawan farmers—the *bo*, for instance, a pole for carrying water, the *sai* a dibble for making holes in the ground for seeds—they were secretly transformed into weapons to oppose the conquering Japanese. The domestic made lethal; that's the legend. The knife, however, is, and always has been, an instrument of cutting. On the dojo floor I hold it in my hand.

I buy into the myth; in a way, I have to. Nobody uses the *bo* or the *sai* as a weapon of attack today. They belong to another time, another era—I can learn their application guilt-free. I am merely delving into history. Of course, if I let my mind wander, which is often a good thing, I can see that a *bo* and a baseball bat may have similar martial application. A baseball bat, benign against a ball, is crushing against a skull. Homeowners hide them under their beds. And baseball itself, the sport I have long loved, acknowledges the bat's potential in a funny kind of way. Why is Frank Thomas, designated hitter for the White Sox, nicknamed the Big Hurt? Because when he hits the ball out of the park, he crushes it. The ball, it might be said, making its way across the sky, sees stars. In black belt class, we practice an overhead *bo* strike to the head and another, diagonal, strike to the temple. Sometimes we say that the arc of the *bo* is similar to that of a baseball bat. I've heard myself say that. I picture the bat slicing through the air, the bat I held in my own hands once, on summer nights when my father tossed a sixteen-inch softball over the sewer cover that doubled as a makeshift plate, and the stars, emerging one by one, dotted the sky overhead, and the point at which, in my mind, the bat makes contact and the ball flies off, that's the point I focus my *bo* strike to the temple. If you do it right, the *bo* whooshes in the air.

So, I am a woman who carries a big stick. There is, I must admit, something pleasurable in that, as if I've turned society, my own small corner at least, on its head. But a woman who carries a knife? That gives me pause. Unlike the *bo*, the knife is not a relic. Its function has not been consigned to history, although, in an impulse both romantic and distancing, I do remember seeing *West Side Story* almost forty years ago, when I was ten, the Jets squaring off against the Sharks, each wielding knives. My mother took me to see that film. I learned the words to *I Feel Pretty*. Like Maria, I primped in front of a mirror. And though, at the end, Maria was reputedly killed by a rival gang member, and Tony, upon learning of her supposed death, inconsolably begs for the same, it is not lost love or feuding factions that is forever fixed in my mind but the Rumble, thrilling, threatening, nimble, acrobatic, accompanied by the chill glint of blades.

THREE YEARS LATER, at thirteen, I bought my first pair of heels. I went up and down Devon Avenue—past Lazar's, Levinson's Bakery, Selma's Deli, Carol Corr—trying on pumps. Finally I settled on plain black, in imitation of my mother, elegant and understated. I wore them to all the bar mitzvahs. People—my mother's friends—said I had a good figure. Six years after that, I went into a downtown sporting goods store for a backpack and a knife. I no longer shaved my armpits. I was going to Costa Rica; the backpack—army green vintage, brown leather straps—was for jeans, D. H. Lawrence's *Lady Chatterley's Lover,* and a six-month supply of sanitary napkins because I was worried I wouldn't be able to get them so close to the equator. The knife was for the pack. Be independent, my mother used to tell me. She meant: *don't worry about what other people say, worry about what I say.* I wasn't sure how to be independent, but I knew how to shop. Knife, pack, map, stamps, flashlight, mosquito repellent: I'd be ready for anything.

It was hard to buy a Swiss army knife; there were so many lined up under the counter, with so many attachments. Did I need a corkscrew? But I hardly drank. A nail file? A pair of those tiny, baby scissors? The knives were beautiful, a dark glossy red, stamped with the signature silver cross. The blades fit snugly inside, each incised with a moonlike notch curved to fit your fingernail. Some of the blades, jaunty with precision, were already pulled out, at the ready. I was hesitant, confused. The salesman waited silently, on the other side of the counter. Suddenly, his silence felt like all the reasons I might need a knife to begin with: as a counter against fear and contempt and scorn and judgment and accusation; something I could put between myself and the world, the world's perceptions of me, and my perceptions of myself. Finally, I chose a streamlined one, with a can opener. It had a tepee-like tent and the word CAMPING etched in silver. I'd never been camping before. The closest I'd come was sleeping next to an open window.

In Costa Rica, I carried the knife with me over the mountains. *Leave me alone,* I learned to say. I practiced under my breath. *Déjame en paz.* But when the police picked me up at two o'clock in the morning—an American woman walking alone on the Inter-American highway—I had no words to explain to myself or them what I was doing. It's my birthday, it's my birthday, I kept repeating in my truncated Spanish, as if that would account for why, four hours earlier, driving back to San José with friends, I'd gotten out of the car and decided to walk, buttressed only by a cautionary phrase and the Swiss army knife in my pocket.

The police held me for several hours. In a nearby town a man had been found dead, and I was, after all, suspicious. I sat in the back seat of their car while they alternately asked questions and ignored me. They talked among themselves in rapid-fire Spanish made more isolating by the frightening circumstances. At one point someone offered me a glass of water and a banana, and although I'd been told to only drink bottled water in Costa Rica, I accepted gratefully. Waiting for my innocence to become apparent, or at least my foolishness—*it's my birthday, it's my birthday*—I felt the weight of the knife sitting in my pocket; I had a weapon, a concealed weapon, on my person, and while I hadn't used it, or used it only as a prop, a lucky charm, the dead man wasn't so lucky. Would I be searched? The knife discovered? Night turned into day, and in the light of dawn the police revealed that the man had not been killed, he had taken his own life, a *suicida*, and though we did not have a shared language to express our subdued relief that life's burdens had not overtaken one of us that night, we fell into a close and oddly comforting silence on the drive back to San José, until one of the policemen turned to me and said, with avuncular consternation, Do not do such a thing again.

I STARTED MY martial arts training in 1991, the day the Persian Gulf War began. Driving to the dojo for my first class, I listened while public radio broadcast the first accounts of American fighter-bombers raiding Iraq. It was early evening in Chicago and already dark; early morning and still dark in Baghdad. The city shook from the force of the explosions, one reporter said. I parked the car, upped the heat; the sky was like a fireworks finale on the Fourth of July, the report continued. I felt afraid, imagining the low flight of planes over *my* neighborhood. Would I be safe in the basement? Then I felt ashamed for hoping the war would stay *over there,* for hoping I could oppose it from a safe distance. We've just bombed Iraq, I said to the person at the front desk, compelled to tell someone a war had started.

During the next few weeks, as the war continued, I learned how to make a fist. Scud missiles landed on Tel Aviv. Turkish soldiers threw frozen chickens at the Kurds, striking many in the head. I'd used my fists one time before, punching a pillow so hard I bloodied knuckles on both hands. You are defeating your weakness, the pony-tailed Gestalt therapist pronounced, as others in the group looked on. Bewildered and humiliated, I never came back. Now I had teachers who instructed me properly. This is your weapon, they said, the first two knuckles at the base of your fingers, the knuckles of your index and middle fingers. This is what will strike your target. On the dojo floor, a polished wood surface overhung with Japanese curtains, called *norens,* the body became a battlefield. There were targets: solar plexus, floating rib, temple. Weapons: spear hand, hammer fist, sword peak, knife foot. We did push-ups on our knuckles to toughen them. What did it mean—did it mean anything?—to study a martial art when American military personnel referred to civilian casualties in Iraq as *collateral damage?* Do not be glib, I told myself. Do not look for easy metaphors. *Kiai,* the instructors said, and on the last punch we yelled—not unlike a war cry—together. The sound, I must admit, was exhilarating.

IN 1982 Ann and I were robbed. We lived in the first-floor apartment of a three-flat. Ann came home first, four-thirty in the afternoon, to find the front door slightly opened. It was stupid, she says. She says that now, but then she walked right in. They took the usual stuff—stereo, jewelry; it's what they left that I remember. Our underpants tossed across the bedroom floor; a knife sitting on Ann's antique walnut dresser. It was our knife, from our kitchen; what I think of as a butcher knife. The robbers had, obviously, carried it around with them, and when they were done, when there were no more goods to be heisted, dropped it on the dresser.

Ann is a cook. By profession she's a graphic designer. She likes tools. She's proficient with a compass and an X-Acto knife. She likes to strip woodwork, owns a spackle knife. On our first date she served me rabbit stew, sort of like beef Stroganoff. It's French, she told me. The knife on the dresser was hers, a Sabatier; French, too. Large, heavy, with a polished black handle. Sabatier is a family name, famous French knife makers, cream of the crop. I didn't know that then.

The police dusted the knife for prints, but when they were done with it we put it back in the kitchen. They never caught the guys or found our stuff, though later we did get some money from the insurance. We called our friends to tell them we'd been robbed. Other than that, we wrote down the serial numbers of electronic and other equipment and put the numbers in an accordion folder labeled *Important Papers*. We went on. We cooked a lot in those days. It was part of our early romance. Russian vegetable tart, popovers, Finnish rusks, croissants, calzones, polenta pizza, zuppa inglese. We grated, peeled, minced, chopped.

In the years since then, we've let our knives grow dull. I don't think it's too harsh to say that, inadvertently, we've abused them. Like life in general, I guess, with equal measures of neglect, despair, surprise, wonder. Over a year ago my great-aunt, age ninety-four, said, I want to buy you something. What do you need? We went into Bloomingdale's, the housewares department. She hung heavily on my elbow. Get what you need, she repeated. The salesman, a handsome Latino man with a name tag that said Carlo, talked about all the knives, Wüsthof-Trident, J. A. Henckels, Sabatier, KitchenAid. Some were factory stamped—and here he took a tone of offhand dismissal—others—nodding in approval—hand-forged high-carbon stainless steel. He spoke with enthusiasm and knowledge, but I couldn't really follow. Which one do you recommend? We sell a lot of these as wedding presents, he pointed. My aunt threw him her winning, blue-eyed smile. Sabatier, I said, the basic set: chef, bread, boning, slicer, parer. Get the sharpener, too, my aunt insisted.

SOME PEOPLE like their knives dull. They feel safer. My friend Elene—not her real name—is that way. She prefers kitchen knives with no bite, no grip; she'll hack away, no matter. Recently, however, she moved to a new city, a new job, and, perhaps in celebration of the fact that she was not required, for the time being, to live a life of vigilant downscaling, bought a new set of knives.

But having bought them, she was afraid. Arrayed on her kitchen counter, they were a hazard. A threat. She moved the knives to an inconvenient corner of the kitchen, a place where she would not have ready access; where she would have to pick one up with deliberation, not impulse. She would break these knives in, but slowly; she would wait for them to become blunt and reassuring.

She told me this over lunch at a café. Her dark eyes had an expression both wry and wounded. When she wasn't looking, I'd noticed how thin her legs were, how she ate her Caesar salad cautiously, almost leaf by leaf, chewing slowly, as if she couldn't quite afford the pleasure of gusto. Dimly, I remembered how years before on a drizzly London street, she'd asked me if I ever felt like giving up, like I couldn't go on. We'd just passed a wall covered with graffiti, *Dance to the Death* slashed across it. I hadn't felt that way, not yet, but I didn't feel immune either. I sensed that her despair could be mine, momentarily. Now, in the café, I thought I knew what Elene was afraid of. Once you have a tool, you're likely to use it. One swipe of the wrist, or two if you want to be sure, that's all it would take. Better to keep the knife at arm's length.

L ET ME SAY something about the knives in my dojo: they're fake. We call them practice knives. Rubber or wood, the blade edge is decidedly dull. The pliant rubber one—this past Christmas I saw a similar version in a toy store, complete with cape and mask— reminds me of Halloween. The wooden knife, smooth, polished, heavy, grained, is beautiful, in its way. We have a weapons wall in our dojo, where the practice weapons, in a show of sincerity, are mounted and displayed; that's where we keep the knives, in an open box, handles amassed in a cluttered array. There are two other knives, not displayed, with tooled leather sheaths and ornate handles, that a student brought back from Africa, as gifts. I've taken them home to look at them. One of the handles is a carving of a woman with a scarified face. Feeling the grooves on the woman's cheeks, I wonder how these cuts are made. With a knife such as this? I run my finger along the blade, unsharpened, and realize, with a start, that for a second I've been lulled into thinking this is a real woman, real flesh. Real knives, we keep these hidden away in the *shinzen,* our dojo altar.

Karate means "empty hand." That's the art I study, the art of the empty hand. First we learn to kick and punch, block and parry, and only after several years of empty-handed practice do we pick up the knife. It's an earned responsibility. Whenever one of our teachers says, Go get a knife, a jaunty nervousness fills the dojo. The knife is the weapon of our nightmares. It is our oldest weapon. Last night Ann dreamed that she was slashed across the back, all the way from her hip to her shoulder. She felt an enormous rush of air and woke up cold and trembling.

We wield the knife in order to learn how to defend against it. To be good defenders we must be good attackers.

I'd never wielded a knife before. Does that sound silly? I wasn't the kind of kid who hid behind a mountain of dirt waiting to vanquish my opponent. I dressed up as a lady on Halloween. Ann played those games; she was that kid. There's a picture of her, four or five years old, skinny as now, with long braids, straight bangs, overalls, a holster at her hips, six-shooters drawn and ready. The expression on her face is one of impish determination. I sat on the couch one night, after a karate class, holding a table knife in my hand. The knife was from the set of flatware I inherited after my father died, but my mother was the one, a long time before, who'd selected it, and I thought of it as somehow reflecting her, stylish and classy. Plain, with a little scrolly flourish on the handle, a matte silver finish, engraved with *International Stainless Deluxe* on the back. I looked at the knife. I felt foolish. I gripped it, not like I was going to cut a piece of chicken or asparagus, but in simulation of a stab. I cried a little, just enough, even though I was alone, to feel embarrassed. Attack with a knife? How was I supposed to know how to do this?

We are very ceremonial with our knives. We are polite attackers. We have rituals of engagement. We bow, display our knives openly so as to harbor no secrets, assume a fighter's stance. I love the bow, I appreciate that moment when I hold the knife, blade down and away from my body, in my extended right hand, left over my heart, and I meet the eyes of my partner, who, earnest and empty-handed, bows back. It is a fundamental gesture. There is a moment before attack.

And then? And then, we're down to business. We learn the language, and mechanics, of attack.

There are grips. Regular grip, blade above the fist; reverse, blade below. Palm to palm, grip to grip. And strikes. Slash, stab. Horizontal, diagonal, left to right, right to left. Over the top, like Norman Bates, in *Psycho*. Our teacher makes a rueful laugh. *A knife strike, in order to be maximally effective, must be delivered with the whole body.* Like this. *Penetrate their space.* Use the hip. It is a wild and awkward choreography, pairs of wide-eyed students skirting around the room, yet even the most inexpert among us occasionally lands a hit.

I feel the knife as it lands, reverberating back in my hand.

Of course, there's defense as well. That's the point, isn't it. Evade, hollow, redirect, disarm. Finish with a disabling blow. We guard with the fleshy undersides of our forearms turned away from the attacker to protect the veins from being slashed.

At the end we bow again.

TAKE AN informal survey. I have a sample of two. What does it mean to fight like a girl? To be uncommitted, Sandi says. To fight like a man means you're not really trying to hit the face; you're trying to hit the back of the head. To fight like a girl means you bounce off. You're cringing. Demonstrating, Sandi throws a wayward punch, her thumb stuck on the inside, and I resist the urge to correct it. She has dark wiry hair I've always envied.

Ann, a martial artist herself, says to fight like a girl means not even fighting. Hitting with the bottom of the fists, she adds, hair-pulling, scratching.

Barbara, who's not part of my survey but knows about hair-pulling and was, in high school, a greaser from Cicero—the Chicago suburb that wouldn't let Martin Luther King Jr. march down its streets—once told me that some of the toughest girls in school ruffed their hair really big and then stuck in razor blades so that if anyone tried to grab them they got a handful.

For my part, I slapped my brother across the face when I was four and he was a baby. On Sunday mornings, our parents sleeping, I waited for Gary to pull himself up by the bars of the crib, his blond head peeking over the top, and then I crawled out of bed in the room we now had to share and slapped him until he stared crying and my father, in his boxer shorts and undershirt, groggily came to console him. When my father left, I hit him again. There's a picture of me then, wild and unkempt, my hair tangled and my dress like the housedress of a beleaguered homemaker. I was snarling at my brother, who's bunched up and smiling in the buggy.

Years later, I resorted to a weapon. Angry for a reason I no longer remember, I dug my braces—a blade of sorts and what I had available—into my brother's forehead, previously unmarked and smooth and pink as porcelain, and hovering over him, both of us splayed atop my parents' bed, I waited for the skin to pull apart, the parallel cuts, small and precise, to widen, the blood to bloom and bead up, the terror, on his face and probably on mine, to spread.

And it did. What could be more terrifying than hurting someone unless, of course, it is being hurt? Does my brother have a scar? I'm not sure. His forehead is high, and his hair, still blond, is receding.

One, two, three, a neighbor, four years older, with half an index finger, a stub I stared at, counted as we walked through Indian Boundary Park one night. The trees interlaced their limbs. Footsteps crunched on the path; they were ours. I knew something was coming. After each number he paused, a gap. I tried to stay one step ahead. I wondered how I had gotten here. My mother played mahjongg with his; even now, I can hear them making their bids.

At *three* his hand, the one with the foreshortened finger, landed on my shoulder.

He didn't hurt me then, but he could have.

Now there's a self-defense poster in the dojo locker room. I look at it while I'm getting dressed. Learn how to fight like a girl, it says, with a picture of a woman, palm heel extended, warding off her attacker. I catch a look at myself in the mirror. My belly, which should be taut from sit-ups—we do them regularly in class—is, instead, like a slab of clay stuck with thumbprints, making me look soft and doughy. I vaguely remember someone saying this is cellulite, and I feel embarrassed, not so much for having it, but for having become, without acceding to it, a cliché. Shaking my head, I turn back to the poster. *Learn how to fight like a girl.* Another cliché, but stood on end. I took a self-defense class once, during a time beset by self-doubt and confusion, when I lived in a faded green apartment above an elderly Italian woman who complained my footsteps were too loud. Once a week for six weeks I aimed my newly formed front kick at an imaginary attacker's knee while at home I padded softly across my living room floor. At the end of the class I was awarded a certificate, and several months later, carting boxes down the stairs, I moved out.

A NN AND I need another paring knife.

This time I go not to Bloomingdale's but to Chef's Catalog. Overpriced, my aunt says, but she's too frail to come with me, and besides I'm a sucker. It's the store for the home chef. When I ask for Sabatier, the saleswoman—late twenties, robust, authoritative, a professional herself, she tells me—says they don't carry that line anymore. Seems that somewhere along the way the company sold its name to anyone who would buy it and it was all downhill from there. She shakes her head with regret but perks up pronto and leads me to the Wüsthof-Trident. They're the best. Before I know it, I've got a paring knife in my hand. Full-tang, no-slip grip. She remarks on the perfect balance.

I ask the price, but it's a diversion. How can I tell her I don't want to buy a German knife? I'm uneasy about German products. When I was a kid, our next-door neighbors were German, and I didn't think anything of it until their dog started barking incessantly across the fence. My father talked to the neighbor, Mr. Bornschlage—by trade a baker who brought home stacks of confections in cardboard boxes—but the dog didn't let up. The Germans have never liked us, my father said, his voice suggesting that this was the final and determining remark in a long, tiresome conversation; by *us* he meant Jews. I practically rolled my eyes because history was history and I was a modern, optimistic child, but I guess now, all these years later, I'm his daughter. In the store, I make an easy connection between cutlery and the Nazis. I'd like to say I already knew about the Night of the Long Knives, also called Röhm's Putsch, the Great Blood Purge, when Hitler ordered the murder of four hundred Brownshirts, but I only learned about that later. Did Wüsthof-Trident manufacture daggers for the SS? The saleswoman moves on to another knife, the J. A. Henckels, but it's a lost cause. Yes, she says, when I ask if both companies are German, in an underhanded effort, I suppose, to point it out to her. Do I think, once enlightened, she'll come around and disavow the product? And they're located in the same town, a block from each other, she adds, like it's a coincidence, but to me it's a conspiracy.

Shamelessly I go on. Have the companies been around a long time? Since before World War II? I'm trying to re-create the lines of historical culpability, but the saleswoman can't help me. By now her uninformed answers have taken on a bemused, cautious tone— uh-oh, this customer is a little loony—and I decide to drop it, exiting with what I know to be a lie. I'll be back, I say. All our cutlery goes on sale at the end of the month, she informs me.

At home I head straight to the kitchen. I'm uneasy. Driving back in the car, I've been plagued by a certain memory. There's another knife, one I bought several years ago, cheap, a manufacturer's special. I bought it at Chef's Catalog. We keep the knives in one of those slanted wooden blocks on the counter, and there in the slots at the bottom, where they always sit, are two paring knives, the hand-forged, high carbon, full tang Sabatier, and the other knife, the one that up until now I'd forgotten, with the flimsy blade—nicked, which is why we need a new one—and molded black plastic handle. I pick it up and look at the logo. J. A. Henckels.

I'm not done. At the library I learn that both Wüsthof-Trident and J. A. Henckels are headquartered in Solingen, a steel town in the Ruhr region. I picture Gary, Indiana, only prettier. There are rolling hills and maybe a child or two in lederhosen. The hills are supersaturated with green. Then I come across a book called *Collecting the Edged Weapons of the Third Reich*. Solingen, the book says, is known as the "city of swords." Most Nazi daggers came from manufacturers located there. I'm smitten, I have to say, by the alliteration—never mind it's a translation—which strikes me as happily convenient, like Solingen and swords were meant for each other, and what's more, I'm about to discover something. I look into the faces of bald-headed master craftsmen in aprons holding knives. Is there guilt; remorse; pride of product? Their eyes are opaque. The book has a list of manufacturers: Carl Eickhorn; Richard Herder; Ernest, Pack, and Sohn; Wagner & Lange; Alexander Coppel; Robert Klass; Karl Böker; C. Bertram Reinhr. There are even several Jewish-sounding names—Jacobs and Company, Joseph Wolf—but surely this is impossible. Yet there is no mention of Henckels or Wüsthof-Trident among the companies that supplied the Nazis with blades. Listlessly, as if exhausted by my spirited but fruitless efforts to assign blame, I turn a few more pages. Under a photo of blown-up buildings, a caption says that Solingen suffered grave damage from Allied bombing during the war. Alone at the library table, I feel rebuked.

TWICE, I'VE GONE under the knife. First a tonsillectomy and later a nose job. Minor surgeries, minor changes to my personal topography. Or maybe not. I have a pert nose, a nose I have long thought of as mine, although I have wondered if, confronted with my old nose—rather bulbous looking, my mother had emphasized—acquaintances or strangers would still say, and here I have noted the slight hint of innocent incredulity, *I didn't know you were Jewish.* This saddens me a bit, because I want to be taken for who I am. I'd like to have something that gives it away. But then I was sixteen and wanted to be loved.

As for the tonsillectomy, well, It doesn't hurt, I told my brother years later when it was his turn, but I must have known that was a lie.

Still, in the long run, I have been more traumatized by cutting than by being cut. I have not, given the opportunities, demonstrated either adequate precision or speed with the knife, and both these skills are at its essence. You're too slow, my mother once said when I was chopping an onion for the meatloaf, and as she grabbed the knife from me, taking my place at the cutting board, I sensed in her an exasperation so deep, so profound, I was helpless. She meant no harm, I tell myself now, recalling the swift fury with which she dispatched the onion. Perhaps she only wanted me to be proficient.

In graduate school, as an exercise physiology student, I took a human anatomy class where, in a basement lab, we dissected cadavers for a semester. I could never, quite, make the cut. I felt like a butcher, raising a scalpel along such rubbery flesh. Here? There are

206 bones in the human body, 29 in the skull alone, and more than 600 skeletal muscles. Where to cut? I would look at the body laid out before me—the body so amateurishly cut—in this case a woman whose pressed lips and bony feet and hands and taut wrinkled neck suggested, to my mind at least, a parsimonious old age, and wonder what in the world prompted her to submit to our fumblings. When she signed up, had she imagined spending her final days under such unsure hands? *Cadaver* is from the Latin for fall, and what a fall it was, upright from the air we breathe prone to this dissecting table, but here she was, all artifice removed, bone and blood and skin and hair and guilelessness. Her faith was overwhelming.

IN THE DOJO LOCKER ROOM, where the conversation not uncommonly turns to targets and weapons, a friend is talking to Ann about the *sai,* the arcane weapon Ann's lately taken a shine to. It's your weapon, the friend says with a nod. Ann demurs, but I know, from where I stand across the locker room that, ever the girl with the six-shooters, she's pleased.

Do *I* have a weapon?

I like the knife. I've gotten, if not good at it, better. I've acquired a certain flair. On occasion I strike with fluency. From across the years I'd tell my mother I can use a knife now, not to cut an onion, no, I am the same as before, slow and plodding, but I use it in a way she never imagined. I aim it at someone, I try to hit that person, although the knife is fake and I am only practicing.

Why? she might ask, and with these twenty years between us since her death what I hear is mostly puzzlement, not accusation or regret.

I know she's referring not only to the knife, but to the fact that four or five times a week I put on my *gi,* that tailored, unstylish white uniform, and kick and punch. From her corner of the room, she might think a *kiai* sounds like an anguished grunt.

She doesn't ask, but I do, Would I ever cut someone? Not myself, my terrors are not those of my friend Elene's, that the knife would make its way across my wrists, although when my great-aunt, ever more frail now at ninety-five, says she would rather hurt herself than hurt me, I know, deep down, what she means.

Why? my mother repeats.

I don't know, I might say, but the truth is I know but don't know how to say it. My body knows.

It's beautiful, I say.

It's necessary.

I want to.

Be careful, she says.

I will, I answer. I am.

NO CUTTING, the Japanese master said, during a senior black belt test, when one of the students, in a symbol of victory and vanquishment, ran the practice knife over her downed opponent's wrist.

No cutting, Kaicho, my teacher's teacher, said again.

Even in the grand theater that the martial arts can sometimes be, he did not want to see the knife wielded for purposes of vanity or revenge.

On another stage, another day, he and his son, the heir apparent, bowed to the crowd at Lincoln Center, the son in a black ceremonial robe, the master in a plain white *gi* and frayed black belt, itself almost turned to white, and while the father retreated to the side, the son, center stage, unsheathed his sword, flashing silver in the lights, and brought it down upon the three-foot tall Japanese daikons flanking the stage, their heads rolling to the floor, while through the crowd rolled too an audible whisper, before he, the son, turned and faced his unarmed father, kneeling on the ground, and after a pause—when not a sound was heard—lowered the sword toward the top of his head, and the master, rising swiftly, clapped his palms together and caught the blade between his hands, and as he unfolded them, like bird's wings to show they were untouched, the audience, myself among them, let loose and applauded wildly.

I have just picked up a man,

a boy really,

and I am not fucking him.
I am driving

my car, not parking,
and I'm taking him

there to the diner
on the other corner.

We will sit and trade names.
He won't tell his real one, but

I'll read to him.
He will shake his head

or nod; he may not understand.
I have just picked up a man

and if he is afraid, he'll talk
or if he is hungry, he'll listen

but either way, I'll read him
some poems, glance at myself

in his eyes, and in the moments
before I drop him anywhere

he wants to go,
neither of us will be alone.

JEFF CRANDALL

Everything Is Phallic When a Man's in Need

We're downing cocktails in a skyscraper.
A fly zips along the long wooden sill.
Below, the Cascade Erection Company
is screwing together a scaffolding
under a pendulous crane.
His name is Dick, Willy or Peter.
I can't remember. He says, "It's hard
to get ahead in bonds." I think
Who are you kidding? We grip our highballs.
The bartender pricks a banana with a knife.
I say, "Cleopatra's Needle shipped on a barge
up the Thames." I say, "Foot-long Kielbasa.
Woody Woodpecker. A mongoose in a cobra hole."
He looks down
and sighs, "Such a stiff drink." Then,
"I like fencing, spelunking and the toboggan."

Ode to Alternative Insemination

Now I am overjoyed at the wetness in my drawers
and the way my ovaries start crowing for attention
at any mention of lesbians
having children!

I read the announcement printed on linen,
knock back my fresh-squeezed breakfast juice
and run into the street to whoop and prance
with my empty glass—

now, I know there are fountains
of sperm going off all over the world,
it's like Versailles out there, Rococo,
24/7, no monuments needed,

it's sheer geysers,
a natural resource,
anonymous,
humble and glorious!

Imagine the plumage in the bathroom stalls,
the public parks! Who needs to pay
doctors for vials in freezers?

My breasts begin to dance
like ecstatic little dogs on their hind legs,
work it on up, boys, high in the air,
and let me catch some!

Shoot into my front yard,
from Paris, from Dallas, from Dakar, from El Salvador,
from an airplane, a rowboat, a car,

I don't care!

Just let me catch some!

CHRISTOPHER MURRAY

Dream of You As Castro with Bad News from the Revolution (and Test Results)

for T. P.

You're Havana to me, baby,
the spirit of exile.
You're my Castro, baby doll,
so long and not yet dead?
Kennedy and Nixon and, God,
everyone in Russia,
you've outlived them all.
Please don't die, Fidel,
promise me that.
I need to know
you're down there,
chomping on your cigar,
hacking through the underbrush
with your machete.
Go, girl.
The salsa in your blood
makes mosquitoes drunk.

My heart is setting on you,
sinking into night.
It's the time
when a man gets tired
of endless revolutions.
When he'd just rather piece
together a meal
at the end of a long day,
cold chicken, plantains,
leftovers,
sit heavily at the old table
and listen to the radio.
Pretty white women
singing *rum and coca-cola.*

His cigar breathes
slowly in the afterdusk.
He should light the lamp
now, he knows, but doesn't.
If he stays tipped
up on his chair,
then tomorrow will never come.
He opens another bottle
of stolen American liquor
and holds some,
the final swallow,
a diamond on his tongue.

It creeps through the blood of our brothers
(young men with hopes and erections)
and glows from within like a tan.
Hearts swell, hearts burst,
hands lose their grip.
Sheer youth protects these boys
for a moment.
Their need like noon,
to shine over all,
leaving no shadows,
to hide or doubt.

The die is cast,
you stupid fuck,
the Cold War's over.
The boys sputter
and fade in hospitals or graves.
Nurses or trees
shade their last brilliance.
They go quietly into music
like dusk. No boys remain,
just ancient you whispering
melodies of booze and greatness.
You are not who you were.
So lift your heart, my Fidel,
sing *Aves* nightly.
Go ahead, light the lamp,
lift the torch,
sing off key.
The disease is in you, Castro.
You're done for now.

LISA VERIGIN

Mabel Takes a Stand

It must have been with pain and anguish that the screen fans
read how Mabel Normand, pictured as a devotee of Voltaire
and Nietzsche, testified that on her way to William Taylor's
house on the fatal night she stopped at a newsstand to buy a
bag of peanuts and copy of the *Police Gazette.*

—*Detroit News,* 9 February 1922

Mabel Normand is a fake! your newspapers said,
all yellow-voiced, soon as Bill was found dead
and I, the last to see him breathe—him who you men
dub a goddamn savior to this dumb comedienne
who wouldn't know Culture if it bit her ass (my head

gone pulp with dope and sensation, y'know), chucklehead
of the stars for thinking life is patchwork a single thread
joins, not whole, plain cloth. (*Sigh.*) Always the same: when
    bland men roam

for trouble, they flash press cards. They yank, snip, shred
the thread. Parts fall apart. Fit the girl in her narrow bed.
Why can't you jokers simply let a girl be human?
Can't she love caviar *and* donuts? Nietzsche *and* G-men
tales? And do you actually think I care if I'm "discredited,"
    you normal madmen?

LISA VERIGIN

Two-Reel Comedy

> I better take my goop because I feel like I'm gonna
> have a little hemorrhage.
>
> —Mabel Normand

Light pours from the machine,

Up the stairs,

That splayed band of white

Through the little chapel

Illuminating dust.

At the heart

So long as the dark remains dark,

Of Calvary Mausoleum,

It is 1915 and you're not ashamed.

Skirting the transept

On the screen,

Into arterial halls,

Within a papier mâché valentine,

Past a tumble of scuffed prayer benches,

A woman's face languidly raises

Past a stack of rotting Barrymores,

To meet your face.

I found her crypt.

Hers is envelope pale,

A clutch of wilting flowers

Shaped by night-colored flows of hair.

Half-obscuring her name, dates,

Her teeth are like thirty-two

Color waning to antique hues

Peppermint drops.

Like the ticky-tack broiling outside

The projector's chirr,

Just beyond the gates.

The only sound.

           As a maintenance man dozed

So long as the dark remains dark,

             At the far end of the hall,

It remains 1915.

         I thought of browned, snapready bones

The slow dope suicide

           And the 1930 frill pink gown

Has not yet begun.

            In which she was interred.

All are still so young ("Younger

        The body is just as fragile as nitrate

Than everyone, wrote Miss St. Johns),

          But burns at a slower dissolve.

Nobody knowing

          I pressed my face to the stone.

Words for "tomorrow."

         A joke repeated in my head:

Yet even in this dark, Mabel's face is

        Some slapstick gag in black and white:

Always too soon consumed by a fade.

        The cold taste of ache in my jawbone.

The name for what we were, archaic today, was Twinkie.
We were Twinkies, moist and pliant confections to gulp in
three bites, welcome sponges to soak in stronger flavors, with
a faint, helpful grit in the aftertaste. Our freshness was hypo-
thetically perpetual. At what point, after all, might a
Twinkie, could a Twinkie shrivel, sour, melt, or fester?

JAMES MAGRUDER

Buccellati

ONE PLACE TO LOOK for a suitable husband in the spring of 1983 was the monthly dance at Columbia University. Suitable meant, among other things, *suited:* we were looking for a junior associate at a law firm, a young bond trader or ad writer or public relations exec with money to spend on above-ground transport, illegal stimulants, and surprises from the better department stores. We wanted a man at least two desks past entry level, preferably with a summer share.

It was late May, and I had been in the city for less than a month. Contrary to my expectations, I had quickly found a job at R. R. Bowker, "the publisher's publisher." I worked for Zoltan Breslau, the man who had invented the ISBN in 1957, but you can't eat prestige. My annual salary was $12,600. I needed nicer shoes. My sublet on Jane Street, brokered through a cousin, would end in September.

David knew where to look for a husband. A college friend who had moved to Manhattan right after graduation while I spent months acidulating as a substitute teacher in the school district of my childhood, David was my initial guide to the city. He had done this thing called "Direct Centering," a human potential "course" that involved weekly sessions of ego reintegration. It wasn't a cult, he wrote to me in Evansville—not that I had asked. Whatever it was, Direct Centering had given him the power to convince me to come to New York, as well as the gumption to change jobs twice in ten months, ask for better tables in restaurants, and talk to strangers.

David called us Snow White and Rose Red, as I was fair and fine-boned, and he was swarthy and strong-featured. Moreover, in the game of love and chance, I was the priss and he was the slut. I resisted the feminine implications of his nicknames; I was now a working stiff with four suits of my own and so tried to rechristen us Nord (short for Nordic) and Med (short for Mediterranean), but the names clunked out like cartoon barbells. We were too young and winsome, David said, to have to worry about being butch or femme.

The name for what we were, archaic today, was Twinkie. We were Twinkies, moist and pliant confections to gulp in three bites, welcome sponges to soak in stronger flavors, with a faint, helpful grit in the aftertaste. Our freshness was hypothetically perpetual. At what point, after all, might a Twinkie, *could* a Twinkie shrivel, sour, melt, or fester?

Owen Teeter called me a Twinkie, decently, hopefully, as he walked me to the at 110th Street subway stop after we'd had enough of the Columbia dance. My phone number was folded into the small triangular pocket of his jeans, just in front of his right hipbone. It was two o'clock in the morning. At last sight, Rose Red was striking hieratic poses in the center of the swarm, his curls swept into the improvised turban of his Amherst T-shirt.

My Amherst T-shirt—husband bait—had stayed in my khakis. David had talked me out of wearing shorts, a mistake. My legs were better than his, and the combination of dried sweat and prickly heat from four hours of dancing made them feel rolled in cracker crumbs. I realized a train might take half an hour to show up, there would be no express stop until Seventy-second Street, and I had no air conditioning. Irritation flowed into the hand I offered Owen. "You can call me," I said. He shot his arms up in a sudden stretch of victory.

Far from being a priss, I was an easy, almost predictable lay, but

Owen wouldn't find that out until the third date, should we get that far. We'd get that far, I grumbled to myself on the platform. I was a blond, baccalaureate Twinkie, and Owen, thirty-one with thinning hair, had my phone number. Sticking to the first man who'd said hello wasn't effective husband hunting, and David would chide me for it. It was like accepting the first job offer, which I had. It was like buying a madras shirt at Lord and Taylor, which I had. "It's the Indiana in you," David would say, shaking his head.

Indiana of me as well to have waltzed with Owen Teeter. Once the crowd discovered that the violin figure in three-quarter time wasn't a false start to the latest British import, the floor emptied with comic haste. Owen held out his arms. I placed my hand on his shoulder and said he should lead. His fingers tapped, then curled around my flank just below my ribs. The trick, Owen half-shouted, was not to lean in. Don't look down, he said. Keep your back straight! As we began to glide to the left, I thought of Edith Wharton, an aigrette in her hair, straightening backs with a thwack of her fan.

We weren't terribly terrific at it, but a waltz with a man was worth a try. Like cold sesame noodles, the culinary sensation of that far-off summer of 1983. Peanut butter mixed with chili sauce, I wrote on a postcard to my mother, hard to imagine.

David was working a plate of them the next day at a Szechuan restaurant off Abingdon Square that we liked.

"Did you go home with anyone?" I asked, launching the postmortem.

He grunted no and cut the glistening cable of noodles with his teeth before speaking. "First I mashed with a lawyer in a window seat. But I sent him off for drinks and ditched him when he started smelling like a hamster."

"A hamster?"

"I had hamsters when I was little, ok? He got excited, it *happens,* and the smell of his personal musk mixed with his Eau Sauvage, made him smell like a hamster. Or hamster shavings . . . perhaps," he finished daintily, a tone at odds with the sight of his chin gilded in swirls of peanut sauce. Rose Red had terrible table manners.

"And then after the lawyer?" I asked.

"I let somebody do me in the bathroom."

I frowned. The first to take his shirt off on the dance floor, David was also the kind of guy who managed to lay a groomsman at every wedding he went to. "Hand or mouth?" I asked.

"What do you think?" he said, his thumb bearing down on some egg roll filaments. David didn't consider hand jobs sex. I did.

"What did this one smell like?"

"What's bugging you?" he asked, but then our entrees arrived. David forked a shrimp off my Triple Delight while I called the waitress back for chopsticks.

As expected, Owen's dossier horrified David. Staten Island. SUNY Binghamton. Five years with the Peace Corps. In Ghana. Owen managed no accounts of any kind. Not even a paralegal, he taught English as a second language to refugees in the basement of St. Bartholomew's Church. His father was a trigonometry teacher, so a trust fund seemed the longest of shots. What was the attraction, David wanted to know. Owen was cute, I replied, he was Irish, and Irishmen made the best sinners. He wasn't afraid to waltz. The hand on my back as we threaded our way out of the dance was reassuring. Owen was courtly, I decided, not a useful observation when David hadn't read Edith Wharton.

When I finished, David tilted his head in a manner familiar to me. I might not adhere to his rulings, but I respected the thinking behind them. "Karl," he said.

"David."

"When are you going to learn how to take a compliment?"

"What do you mean?" I asked, flushing. I knew where he was headed.

"What I mean is, you're not under any obligation. A stranger comes up to you and says he thinks you're a beautiful man."

"I shouldn't have told you that," I whispered.

"I admit you were alone and vulnerable, I was off scoping—"

"Mashing."

"I apologize, but still."

"But still what?"

He sighed. "You can just accept the compliment. Say thank you and leave it at that. You don't have to sleep with him."

"I didn't sleep with him! I don't just sleep with people." I also did-n't let people "do" me.

"You have to own your beauty, Karl."

I eyeballed the restaurant in a panic. Where was the hissing wok looking to scar us with hot oil, the poisoned scallion hiding in a pan-cake, the thrown cleavers spinning towards our ears?

"We'll be trolls before you know it," I hissed.

David dropped his empty sugar packets into my teacup. "Exactly my point."

"You don't even want to meet a man," I said with as much spite as I could muster. He laughed and suggested spumoni on Perry Street.

I WORKED IN A building at Sixth and Forty-sixth, a couple of blocks from Rockefeller Center, where I would go and marvel at my right to eat lunch in the crowd. I didn't much take after him, but I fanta-sized that first summer in Manhattan that I was retracing my father's steps. In the early sixties, he had worked in midtown as an account-ant for the Sealtest Dairy Company. I carried his first briefcase, a sim-ple zippered portfolio with frayed handles, his initials in gold long rubbed off the leather by the second knuckles of his right hand, and I fancied that he might be watching me as I bought fruit from street vendors, made bus transfers, carried home the dry cleaning, and signed chits for scotch-and-sodas.

As for what I did when the sun went down—well, my father had died while I was a sophomore and to that date, there had been sig-nals, but no proof of my preference. Had I thought about it, I sup-pose I would have hoped the dead went to bed by ten, which was the hour David and I might begin to contemplate our plumage for the club-crawl to come. Or perhaps my father turned his gaze from my follies to revisit the haunts of his youth, the high-toned nightclubs and low-down bars where he had entertained clients during the June moon of Keynesian economics.

One thing was certain: my father would have been bored stiff to watch me work. R. R. Bowker's most glamorous product was and remains *Publishers Weekly.* I was part of the team that compiled and

maintained the database known as *Ulrich's Serials,* a comprehensive list-
ing of all the magazines known to man. I was the German editor, hired
to sort through the piles of new Zeitschriften sent to Bowker, classify
them, and devise entries consisting of their title, their editors in chief,
their frequencies, and, very occasionally, a one-sentence précis of their
mission. *Advances in Metallurgical Spectography* said it all, while a fashion sheet titled *The Blink of an Eye* required my mindful explication. It
was big news if a magazine changed its frequency: monthly to quarterly, or semiannual to annual. If an annual declined to the status of a
biannual, it was expunged from the database. I myself would place the
weekly list of German casualties on Zoltan Breslau's desk and nod in
sympathy to his pained sighs.

These professional excitements were actually some weeks away.
When I started at Bowker, the newest database feature was phone
numbers for the American serials. The forthcoming *Ulrich's* had a
hard June 15 deadline, so for my first month on the job, eight hours
a day, I entered thousands of ten-digit phone numbers. Nine strokes
of the tab with my left pinkie took me to the area code field, the
tenth to the exchange field. Hit enter and clear. The novelty of using
a computer faded faster than a nosegay of violets. I took no pride
from the fact that I could enter roughly twelve times more numbers
in a day than my office mate Tana Waldman, who had started at
Bowker the week before me. I was simply the faster of two chimps.

After twenty-three years teaching high school Spanish in Ben-
sonhurst, Tana said she was ready to make a mark in the field of publishing. Tana made me nervous. Her purse remained in her lap at all
times, and she gripped it shut with both hands whenever she stood
up. On her desk she had placed a Ziggy statue that said "You're the
Bestest," and she stored rubber bands in a red crystal apple. The
slightest change in the routine—different-colored printout, a new
pass code, a blinking cursor—could derail her completely. For Tana,
each magazine was a brand new world. My attempts to help her log
on, my suggestions that she count tabs instead of reading the screen,
were always met with a defiant, "Yes, I know that." I got used to saying, "Did you hit enter?" when I heard her fingers stop and her
breathing get louder. If we ever finished with the phone numbers,

Tana would be in charge of Mexico and Central America.

"Karl Hedstrom," I said, picking up the phone one Monday morning. From the corner of my eye, I could see Tana leaning intently into her terminal, as if there were aliens within beckoning to make her their queen.

"Good morning Karl. This is Owen Teeter. From the dance." (Snow White, typically, only gave out her office phone number.)

"Owen, I'm glad to hear from you," I said truthfully.

"Would you like to have dinner with me?"

I laughed. "You know how to surprise a girl, don't you?"

We decided to meet that Thursday at the Cupping Room Cafe. After hanging up, I tightened the knot on my tie and opened my weekly minder. I loved filling up its rectangles.

"You're a gay guy, aren't you?"

I looked over at Tana. She was rubbing a spot on her screen with a putty-colored handkerchief.

"Yes, I am, Tana," I said, amazed by her powers of detection. David and I screeched at each other by phone at least twice a day. David was working for an ad agency with more queers in it, he said, than a library school.

"You're fast with your fingers, too," she asserted. It was the first time Tana had acknowledged any difference in our ability to keystroke. I didn't know what to say.

"How many phone numbers did you enter last week, Karl?"

I shot out my cuffs. "They're not keeping track, Tana. They're really not," I lied. We were already known as the Tortoise and the Hare.

"Yes, I know that." I flipped a page of printout. She flipped a page of her printout. "I did seven hundred and thirty-seven last week," she continued, goading me. "So my productivity has increased."

"I should say so," I replied heartily. "Way to go, Tana."

"How many did you do, Karl?"

I halved my figure, then shaved off another hundred. "About thirteen hundred, give or take fifty."

I rolled backward in my chair to give us room. After a moment, as I pretended to locate something essential in my briefcase, I thought I heard her say, "I'm gaining on you, gay guy."

Working from an outdated Zagat's, David had given me the wrong price range for the Cupping Room. Refusing an appetizer *and* a glass of wine *and* dessert would have been strange on a first date, so I wound up five dollars short on my half of the tab. As Owen's guest, I could duck it, but I felt bound to display some independence. The trouble was, my American Express account was all of three weeks old, so the options of splitting the bill with a card and cash, or paying with my card and pocketing Owen's share, exceeded my level of sophistication.

Owen drew first on his wallet; I said oh, let me put it on my card; thumbing bills, he said absolutely not, he'd asked me to dine; I said don't be silly, why don't I just give you these three tens and we'll figure it out later. At that, he struck the edge of the table with four fingers and said with unmistakable temper, "No half-measures, Karl. If I'm buying you dinner, I'm buying you *all* of it."

I was a rube. David and Edith Wharton and my father could say amen to that, but I got even by putting out that night on Jane Street, two dates ahead of schedule.

The next morning, when I opened my eyes, Owen was sitting cross-legged to my left, staring down at me. "What?" I said, rather sharply.

He smiled as a little boy might. "I was just imagining what it would be like to wake up, go to the mirror, and have your face looking back at me."

I groaned and flung an arm over my eyes. He pulled it away, and I pulled him down to shut him up.

So that's how a courtly English language instructor became my first New York, three-nights-a-week boyfriend. There was no other option for Snow White. After a time, the flow of his compliments, supported by the movements of his body, ceased to embarrass me. Owen Teeter was fantastic in bed, which was the trump I played whenever Rose Red hooted to hear that I was turning down another investigation of the newly opened Boy Bar in order to play bridge with Owen and his friends. Bridge, it was true, was the apogee of

Indiana, but I'd air enough gamy details about what else was in me to bring things to a draw over the sesame noodles at Sung Chu Mei.

Owen was the first man I'd slept with who let things occur, rather than made them happen. He was circumspectly, offhandedly *collusive* in a way I came to find irresistible. He brought dessert into bed. He brought me into the shower. He'd suggest I not wear underwear. I'd unzip and find him in a jockstrap. We'd stand. We'd stand in front of a mirror. He'd rut. Or he'd take his time. Or he'd really take his time. He'd talk about it when we weren't having it, then change the subject. Baby steps, but ones we all take. Owen's gift for making sex seem terribly dirty yet perfectly banal was liberating. I knew I had turned some kind of corner when, one day at Bowker, I reminded him over the phone to buy some more lube.

"Yes dear," he said dryly, letting me discover the moment.

"Wait. Did I just say that?"

"Yes, dear. Now, would that be flavored or nonflavored?"

I hung up, amazed at my dirty, banal, sluttish, housewifely self. I resquared my haunches on my chair. I smiled to hear Tana jabbering in Spanish with Josefina, the coffee cart lady. The thought of Owen riding the subway down to Fourteenth Street with a drugstore bag on his lap made for a tumid afternoon with *Ulrich's Serials,* Deutsches division.

OWEN WOULD ALWAYS be taking the subway. That was the tradeoff. He didn't seem to care about money, a philosophy so at odds with Manhattan living as to be pre-Columbian. And this was back when it only cost twenty dollars to leave your apartment. As for his apartment, I ducked David's every question. Owen had a room on the ninth floor of the Greystone Hotel, an SRO at the southeast corner of Ninety-first and Broadway. (Joseph Mitchell territory, but I hadn't read him yet.) Even at high noon, light stopped at the glass entrance doors, so the yellowing mirror tiles on the walls reduced everyone in the lobby to lumbering ochre phantoms. The reception desk was covered with greasy, peeling contact paper. Taped inside the elevators were pictographs showing how to outwit roaches, rats, and silverfish. The water-stained wallpaper in the ninth floor hallway, a repeating toile of the Betsy Ross House and Independence Hall, barely kept truce with the quince-colored shag carpet that squished underfoot and gave off smells of dishrag and fumigant.

Owen wasn't embarrassed by his room, so neither was I. Housing in New York was always impossible, so I guess I assumed that like his job, the apartment was an improvisation until something better opened up. He must have had more than a hotplate, yet I don't recall taking any meals there beyond bagels with the paper. I remember running gear slung over the shower bar, and his running shoes hanging outside by their laces from a cup hook twisted into the grimy windowsill. The ironing board was out a lot, since he was fastidious about his shirts. It was something the Africans had expected of Peace Corps schoolmasters. I remember the bed frame was bolted down, the stress fractures and divots in the wall around the headboard attesting to decades of strong fucking. It was louche, but larky. Owen might look up from the board, meet my eyes, and swagger back for more. I liked that there was never more than two feet to cross to get to what needed to be done. Sex and ironing and reading and coffee and pissing and sleep were all of a piece.

At night, cradling me, rubbing my scalp with his chin, he would apologize for how much he talked. He said he had begun to store up new thoughts for me. Most of the time I held my tongue—it is the Twinkie's prerogative to have nothing to say—but one muggy June night, Owen coaxed me into an historical discussion, meaning the five-week history of us.

I told him about Snow White and Rose Red, and how at first sight I had thought he was Latino and how that had made me nervous. I said I had enjoyed the waltz. I made him laugh when I recalled how a seven-dollar appetizer at the Cupping Room almost sank our relationship. Then, thinking to reassure Owen that I liked how things were, I voiced some of David's milder misgivings about his prospects.

He pulled away and flipped on the reading light. He bent over the nightstand and from its second drawer withdrew a bundle of green felt tied around the middle with a braided bow. He laid it out like a

tiny shrouded body on his pillow, then adjusted the arc of the lamp.
I sat up. He untied the ribbon, unrolled the cloth, and laid open a
flap. There was a quick gleam of tines and crescents.

Six of the eight pockets in the cloth were tenanted. "Silver," I
said. "Family?"

He shook his head. "It's Buccellati," he said. "As they do with
everything else, I believe the Italians make the most beautiful silver in
the world."

He slid a dinner fork from its chamber and closed my hand
around it.

"It's really heavy," I responded, idiotically.

"It's an Art Nouveau pattern, hand-cast and chased, all made to
order. The craftsmanship is the same as it was generations ago."

"It's beautiful, Owen, no, no, it's absolutely gorgeous. It suits you."

He paused for a moment to stroke my knee and lay his head there.
"This is all I have so far. I buy it piece by piece."

I looked down his back to the pair of hollows at the base of his
spine where I liked to press my thumbs. The wheezing air condi-
tioner in the window changed keys. I felt his jaw working against my
knee as he raised his voice above it.

"If I wanted to, Karl, I could fly to Saudi Arabia next week. I could
teach English to the royal children for an obscene amount of money.
I could live in the palace. But right now I want to be in America."

"I know you do," I stuttered, cutting him off, "and I for one am
glad you're here."

"Italians," he sighed, leaning back again to replace my fork with a
soup spoon. "I can afford two pieces a year."

"A semiannual," I replied automatically.

I didn't get it, and he knew it. He placed each piece in my hand,
hoping I'd get it. (Very Helen Keller, David would later say.)

"I do want things, Karl," he said, not looking at me anymore. "It's
just that I'm able to wait for them one at a time."

"HAPPY GRINGO DAY," said Josefina, making change on her afternoon pass-through. The warp of her wish so tickled me, I tipped
her a dollar for my muffin. My heart was light. I was going away for

the Fourth of July weekend. Tucked behind my office door was a new burgundy leather duffel. Inside that was a black leather shaving case, a giveaway for opening a Macy's charge. My hostess gift was a slim 1948 edition of *Contract Bridge Made Easy*, filled with droll line drawings of women in hats.

Owen was poor, but his friend Jay Strickert, a Peace Corps alum with a trust fund, had a house on the Jersey shore. Jay's apartment on Sutton Place, the grandest I'd yet seen, was where we went for bridge. My first time there, something stopped me in the foyer. Beyond the hallway, across a drawing room, between two sets of French doors leading to a balcony was a brooding, blocky painting, a portrait depicting the idea of a king. It was another New York first—textbook art in private hands.

"God, I love Soutine," I said recklessly. "He's one of my favorite twentieth-century artists."

"Thank you, it's a Rouault," said my host.

(It wasn't as if I said I loved his Mondrian, I bitched later to Owen. Art historians always pair Soutine and Rouault.)

The rich were supposed to be sleek, and graceful about setting everyone at ease. Jay had a lumpy body and a spiny temperament. Our fourth at bridge, Tony Neville, was my first link to the pre-Stonewall era. He had hitched to New York from eastern Montana at seventeen. A besotted agent got him into the Actors Studio and managed a nice stage career for him. In the sixties, he'd had a lucrative second run in print ads, and now he sold space in a Jewish cemetery. I secretly regarded Tony as a template for what I'd hoped I could do with New York. I enjoyed playing the acolyte—the Merman versus Martin stuff—with him, Owen smiling over the table at each discriminating question I posed. The Peace Corps queers seem to have skipped right to Sylvester.

From the moment my duffel jounced the bed in our guest room and I lifted Owen into the air, the weekend was my first taste of a different district in the gay community. David had Roxy, the Saint, and the Piers on his holiday docket. I was on the fresh-chervil side of the street. Friday night we grilled steaks as the sun set over Spring Beach. Jay, who could afford to be ironic about our surroundings, was hilarious on the topic of his family. He skewered each photo in a graveyard of silver frames resting on a Steinway until we were helpless with laughter. Collusive Owen lured me onto the dock about three in the morning, and we rocked with a silver moon rippling on the waves.

After a few hours on the beach Saturday, Tony and I went into town for lobsters and strawberries and farm eggs for homemade mayonnaise. We left Jay and Owen reading on the porch, *Contract Bridge Made Easy* riding the swell of Jay's sun-smudged belly.

Jay got mean at dinner. He started by mocking the way Owen shared his claw meat with me. Then he ridiculed Owen's bedsit until Tony shushed him. When I started to clear the dishes for dessert, Jay put his fist on his plate and said that Twinkies didn't have to do anything.

"I'd like to do my part," I mumbled to the discard bowl of artichoke leaves.

"Twinkies don't have a part," he scoffed. "They don't have to clean or cook or drive. They don't clear dishes. Twinkies have one part, and it better be stiff."

"Enough, Jay," said Owen.

Jay set a napkin ring spinning on his forefinger. The lobster juice from his plate dribbled down his arm. "They only have to put out," he insisted, cracking himself up with his visual.

"I might be a Twinkie," I said, "but I'm not a gold digger."

"No shit," he snickered. Owen, at the sink, bit a nail. "Now if this were Africa, Blondie, it would be different." Jay oogled the wine, but Tony was quicker on the draw. He shrugged and wedged the napkin ring like a monocle between his brow and doughy cheek. "If this were Africa, I'd be the bwana, and you'd be my houseboy. You'd have to beat my clothes on a rock. Cook for me, repair my netting, brush my hair, boil my drinking water. You'd brush bwana's teeth if he asked."

"Why don't we get some air?" said Owen. Jay waved his arm to nix the suggestion. His monocle fell and dinged against the lobster hull on his plate.

"And you'd be so grateful for those nine stinking American dollars *a month,* you would service your bwana in every way. Of course, you're too old to be a houseboy. You're past it. Isn't that right, Owen? Don't you think Blondie here is a couple of harvests older than Daga was?"

"This isn't the place for this, Jay," said Owen. He shut off the tap.

Jay turned back to me. "We never knew exactly how old Daga was, Blondie." He swept his plate to the floor; some silver went with it.

Owen was leaning, face-out against the counter, his fingers pushed into his temples, as if a mesmerist's pose could will Jay to silence.

"I don't know," Jay continued, "I suppose we should have split the tab, Owen. Each of us could have paid him four-fifty. A dollar-twelve a week for services rendered. Daga didn't mind double duty, did he? Young and smooth as he was."

At that, Owen whipped past me and dragged Jay out of his chair. Despite the fifty-pound difference, he pushed him out the kitchen door. Their shouts trailed to pips, and then it was just the roll of the waves again.

Tony and I did the dishes, then repaired to the music room for brandy. Drawing upon what he had learned from Harold Clurman, Tony began to play solitaire, a trivial activity that masked his serious intention, which was to tell me that Owen had come back to the United States to find himself a husband. My crew cut was two days old, so my trivial activity was to take delight in rubbing the back of my head against the nap of the velvet couch. "Owen's a great guy," was all I would allow.

"He's aces, Karl. I don't want him to go back to Africa."

I thought of a young black man standing forlornly outside a grass hut. Holding my father's briefcase. "If he can't find Daga," I said, "he could go to Saudi Arabia and make a fortune."

Tony chuckled, another feint. "They put queers to death over there."

I followed the skitter of a daddy longlegs along the picture rail above his head. "Wow," I said, "that's insane."

I picked up the other bridge deck and suggested double solitaire, which I hadn't played since I was a kid in Evansville. Then I got him started on Mabel Mercer, of whom I'd only just become aware. When Jay and Owen got back, we ate shortcake in silence. That night, the next morning, and twice the next day—Gringo Day—I made sure the sex we had was almost comically noisy since Jay's room was next to ours.

"WHAT SUIT are you wearing today?"
"The seersucker."
"God, I love you in that. The pink tie?"
"I prefer to think of it as 'dusty rose.'"
"Of course, lover," said Owen lightly.

I bared my teeth. Since our weekend in Jersey, he had begun slipping that word in, and I'd been letting it pass. I scribbled "lover" on my blotter to remind myself to ask David how to finesse my way out of it.

"Can you knock off at four?" he asked.

"Sure," I said, with the breeze of Zoltan Breslau. "What's up?"

"Meet me at 46 East Fifty-seventh Street, between Madison and Park. That's the south side of the street," he added—unnecessarily. I knew my odds and evens.

Before I left to meet him, there was a crisis at work. The office manager, a retired Fosse dancer with a two-foot braid, brought in a plastic tub and set it down directly in front of me, rather than next to my terminal. Atop a fresh pile of German periodicals was my nameplate. Karl Hedstrom, twelve white letters against a black wood-grain finish.

Given the brain-blanching level of the work I did, it hadn't occurred to me that a nameplate was on its way. This was a milestone, something grave was in order, indeed I felt my father winging close, the nearly forgotten timbre of his voice prompting me to issue thanks to the world of work, but the moment felt silly to me, ridiculous even. "Where did this come from?" was the best I could do. To cover my awkwardness I picked the thing up and slowly traced the grooves with a reverent forefinger.

Tana Waldman stood up; for the first time, her purse fell to the floor. She stepped over it and blocked the open door with her body. According to the office manager, Tana's nameplate had been delayed for "explainable" reasons she wouldn't explain. Tana kept repeating that she had been an employee of R. R. Bowker forty hours longer than Karl Hedstrom, so where was her nameplate?

The tension was so awful, I weakly offered that "H" came before "W" in the alphabet. Tana stamped her heel and snarled, "Yes, I know that," but wouldn't let the office manager out of the room. As she grew more strident, the other members of the *Ulrich's* group gathered a couple of yards beyond the door. When things became too gruesome, after Tana revealed how much she had spent the previous summer on a publishing skills course, how much she had spent on her business wardrobe, how hard she had looked for a job, how involved her commute was, and how proud she felt to be part of the Bowker family, they ducked their heads and peeled away.

Owen was waiting for me in his one suit, an olive worsted from Tripler's, custom-made, and his best tie, Hermès. He was bobbing with happiness at my approach. I wished, and not for the first time, I could be what he saw.

"We're such a handsome couple," he said, kissing me on Fifty-seventh Street.

"This isn't the Village," I said.

"I don't care, beautiful. They know me here," he said, tilting his head toward the vitrine of the Buccellati boutique.

They did know him at Buccellati. He was too excited to notice the quick play of eyes around the horseshoe of cases as he bid the staff good afternoon. He stated his intention to purchase his first dinner knife, his voice beating against the cushioned quiet. And what pattern have you, asked a face tightened with surgeries. I should be in the register, he replied airily. She pretended for several minutes that he was not in the register. When Owen gave the name of his pattern, she pretended not to understand his pronunciation.

I thought of that small green roll in his nightstand drawer, and decided to defend my boyfriend against this covey of Continental closet-cases, gray about the temples, and black-shingled spinsters from the Dalmatian Coast. I wished to remind them that the root

word for service is *servant.* Keeping my mouth sealed, I dropped my
jaw, let my eyelids droop, and placed them all in the middle distance.
I ignored offers of assistance and picked up their catalog as if it were
coated in motor oil. I glanced at two pages and sniffed "zu Barock-
stil" to no one in particular. I recall sneering at an arrangement of
sauce boats as well.

Seated on the couch, I twitched my crossed left foot. Owen
buzzed about the cases looking for a piece of his pattern until he recognized, then drew the mocking attention of the man who had han-
dled his most recent transaction.

"Ah, of course, *signor,* the cream soup spoon," the salesman finally
said, tilting a palm upwards.

"Yes, the cream soup spoon of November last."

"You are ordering à la carte, no?"

"À la carte all the way," grinned Owen.

I could have smote them both for that exchange.

Snow White couldn't be budged from her throne, so at Owen's
urging, the salesman lay a square of green cloth and the knife before
me on a mahogany tea table. It had a French blade. It was superb; it
was exquisitely heavy, timelessly weighty. It could pay for two and a
half months of my sublet. I made some calculations: sometime in the
early years of the twenty-first century, Owen would own enough
Buccellati flatware to host a dinner for six in his room on the ninth
floor of the Greystone Hotel, provided the salad forks could double
for dessert.

"It's quite lovely," I said in a bored fashion to the middle distance.
I placed my hand on Owen's forearm to signal my approval, but the
excitement in his eyes had gone.

Why was I acting like that, he wanted to know when we were outside again.

"Acting like what?" I said. The reaction of the Buccellati sales staff
to his twelve one-hundred-dollar bills had beggared description. I
had wanted to spear their eyes with pickle forks.

"Like you were beyond it all. You were horrible to those people,
Karl."

"*I* was horrible?"

"I was embarrassed for you," he said.

I was so stunned, I walked into a parking meter. "You were embarrassed? *You* were embarrassed? For me?"

To this day I don't know whether Owen was aware of their misconduct, or knew and chose to ignore it. At the time, the rage I felt for having my behavior misinterpreted eclipsed my shame for having spoiled his rarest—and dearest—pleasure.

To PRETEND THAT we could travel through a quarrel, we went for brunch the next day at the Hungarian coffeehouse up by Columbia. It was miserably hot. They were out of the babka, and it was the day I learned I hated kasha varnishkes. Owen didn't understand my ambivalence surrounding the arrival of my nameplate or my confused feelings about Tana Waldman and her mark in the field of publishing. He said this was because I never talked about work, I never talked in general, which was my cue to grow captious about everything. Finally, rather than pin it all on him, kasha included, *his* suggestion, I shut down.

On the walk back down Broadway, Owen made up for my silence with cheery, dispassionate anecdotes about African heat, thereby releasing me to contemplate why I had gone to Jay Strickert's apartment the night before. Why had I taken a cab to Sutton Place at 9:45? Why had I given my name to the desk attendant? Why had I expected Jay to be home? Why, after he'd shut the door behind me, did I unzip my fly in the foyer and give him my stiff part to suck, watching the Rouault monarch on the faraway wall?

Having reached the southeast corner of Ninety-first Street, I slumped against the Greystone Hotel and stared at the traffic island until my vision blurred. Owen asked me if I wanted to go upstairs. I shook my head. Did I want to walk in the park? Nap in the park? Catch a movie? Go to a museum? Nap at home? Meet up later? So many things to do in New York.

I shook my head against all his suggestions and squinted into the sun. The light burned tangents along the tops of my eyeballs and into my brain. All my information could leach out along the edges of these flaming arrows and sizzle to ash and vapor on the sidewalk if I so chose, but the heat and the light and the smell and his gaze—and maybe even the noise, I prayed—stopped three feet to my right.

Owen spoke again.

"Sometimes, Karl, I think you've got a life going on inside that I know nothing about."

If I stretched out my arm, I could cool my fingertips in the shade. And if I stood perfectly still for another ninety minutes, I could disappear into it altogether.

CONTRIBUTORS

CYNTHIA RAUSCH ALLAR has had poetry published in *New Millennium Writings*, *The Underwood Review*, and *Aethlon: Journal of Sport Literature*, among others. Currently reading and influenced by Henri Cole, Rafael Campo, Mark Doty, Adrienne Rich and Marilyn Hacker. Flower: Rose.

ROBIN BECKER, Professor of English at Penn State University, honors French painter Rosa Bonheur whose life inspired Becker's poetry collection *The Horse Fair*. Favorite flower: May Apple.

FRANK BIDART's new book of poetry, *Star Dust*, will be published in June. A Chancellor of the Academy of American Poets, he is the recipient of many awards, including the Wallace Stevens Award. He teaches at Wellesley College in Massachusetts.

SOPHIE CABOT BLACK is the author of two collections of poetry: *The Descent* (2004) and *The Misunderstanding of Nature* (1994), which received the Poetry Society of America's Norma Farber First Book Award. She teaches at Columbia University and divides her time between New York and New England. Favorite flower: the lilac.

LUCY JANE BLEDSOE'S most recent novel is *This Wild Silence*, and her essay collection, *The Breath of Seals: adventures in fear and grace*, will be out next year. Her favorite flower is the columbine. She loves Willa Cather and James Baldwin, and studies Alice Munro (who is not a lesbian) nearly every writing day.

ELIZABETH BRADFIELD lives in Alaska and works as a naturalist and writing instructor. She favors alpine flowers, particularly chocolate lilies and gentians, and has recently fallen for the poems of Ruth Schwartz and Spencer Reece.

JERICHO BROWN is a student in the Ph.D. program in Literature and Creative Writing at the University of Houston, where he studies with Mark Doty and teaches the poetry of Essex Hemphill. His poems have appeared in *Callaloo*. and his favorite flower is the Audrey II.

JAMES CIHLAR's poems have appeared in *Prairie Schooner*, *The James White Review*, and *Briar Cliff Review*. Cihlar reports, "I recently finished Carl Phillips's Coin of the Realm. So many valuable ideas in this poetics book, including his analogy of the lyric poem as the torso of the body, with the head and limbs being supplied by the reader." With his partner, he has nearly succeeded in replacing all of their small lawn with plantings, and counts zinnias and cosmos as favorites. By 2006, he hopes to permanently retire their lawnmower.

TEE A. CORINNE's published work includes *The Cunt Coloring Book* (1975), *Yantras of Womanlove* (1982), and *Dreams of the Woman Who Loved Sex* (1987), and *Intimacies* (2001), which was a Lambda Literary Award finalist. She received the Women's Caucus for Art President's Award in 1997 and the Abdill-Ellis Lambda Lifetime Achievement Award in 2000. Her influences include lesbian photographer Berenice Abbot and bisexual photographer Ruth Bernhard. Her favorite bloom is the gardenia.

ALFRED CORN is the author of nine books of poems, most recently *Contradictions* (Copper Canyon, 2002), a novel, and a collection of critical essays. This year he holds the Amy Clampitt Residency in Lenox, Massachusetts. "I am currently reviewing four collections of critical prose and memoir by John Ashbery, Richard Howard, James Merrill, and Edmund White. I've learned from all four of these, and would otherwise list Whitman, Crane, and Elizabeth Bishop as important influences. My favorite flowers: dogwood, lilac, tiger lily, delphinium."

JOAN COX: "I grew up in a family of artists in Baltimore, Maryland, where I live and paint in a warehouse studio in the city. I am drawn to both the simplicity and complexity of nature, particularly in flowers. My favorite flower is a traditional Southern white magnolia."

JEFF CRANDALL is a Seattle poet who makes his living as an artist combining poetic text with glass. His poems have appeared in *Beloit Poetry Journal*, *Cream City Review*, *Cutbank*, and *The Seattle Review*, among others. His first book, *The Grief Pool*, is published by Firestorm Press. The most influential queer poet on his work is Peter Pereira. Jeff's favorite flour is whole wheat, and his favorite inflorescence is a zigzag path between the Passionflower and the Himalayan Blue Poppy.

EMILY GROPP currently lives in Pittsburgh. Her favorite flower is the morning glory. Queer writers of great influence: Bishop, Rukeyser, Jordan, Rich, and Baldwin.

AMY GROSHEK lives in Anchorage, Alaska. Her first and greatest queer influence is Adrienne Rich. Her favorite "flower" is the pitcher plant, Sarracenia purpurea.

CAROL GUESS is the author of four books, most recently *Femme's Dictionary*. She cites Rebecca Brown, Carole Maso, and Letta Neely as significant influences. The Chihuly Rose is her favorite flower.

JULIE HALL's fields of lupine have appeared in *The Nation* and *The Threepenny Review*. Her queer poet influences include Bishop, Rich, Swenson, Doty, Gunn, Rukeyser, and Kay Ryan. She cofounded progressivekid.com.

MICHAEL HYDE's debut story collection *WHAT ARE YOU AFRAID OF?*, which includes "Life Among the Bulrushes," was awarded the Katherine Anne Porter Prize in Short Fiction and will be published in December 2005. He is an assistant professor at the Fashion Institute of Technology, where he teaches writing and literature. Influential writer: Cather. Influential flower: the azalea; it's hearty, ballsy, and shameless in its beauty.

BILL JACOBSON lives in New York. His work is in the collections of the Guggenheim Museum, the Metropolitan Museum, the Whitney Museum, and many others, and he is represented in New York by Julie Saul Gallery. His favorite authors are Paul and Jane Bowles. Favorite flowers are those given to, and received from, friends.

CHARLES JENSON works for the Piper Center for Creative Writing at Arizona State University, where he edits their biannual magazine "Marginalia." Recent work appears in *MiPoesias*, *Gihon River Review*, and *Portland Review*. He's been most influenced by Frank O'Hara, Jim Elledge, and D. A. Powell; his favorite flowers are honeysuckle and oleander.

RUDY KIKEL is the author of three books of poetry (*Lasting Relations, Long Division,* and *Period Pieces*) and editor of the Gents, Bad Boys, and Barbarians anthologies of gay male poetry. "Sobriety" is a set of nine poems that contributes to a book of 81 syllabic poems entitled *Talks in the Blue*, which is forthcoming from Windstorm Creative. "Early influences on my poetry? The strongest would be work by Richard Howard, James Merrill, Frank Bidart, Dennis Cooper and Edward Field. Favorite flower? Freesia."

JOAN LARKIN is the author of four collections of poetry, most recently, *Cold River*. She was co-editor of the legendary anthology, *Gay & Lesbian Poetry in Our Time* (St. Martins, 1988) and editor of *A Woman Like That: Lesbian & Bisexuals Writers Tell their Coming Out Stories* (Avon, 1999). She is the poetry editor of *Bloom*. Her current favorite flower: the morning glory.

AMY LOWELL was born on February 9, 1874, in Brookline, Massachusetts. Her first poem was published in the *Atlantic Monthly* in August 1910, and she published her first book, *A Dome of Many-Coloured Glass* in 1912. After being included in the first anthology of imagist poets, *Des Imagists* (1914), she edited the annual anthology *Some Imagist Poets* from 1915 to 1917. In addition to her many books of poetry, she published two books of criticism and a biography of John Keats. She died of a stroke on May 12, 1925. The actress Ada Dwyer Russell, her companion since 1909, oversaw the posthumous publication of Lowell's work, including *What's O'Clock*, which won the Pulitzer Prize in 1926.

JAMES MAGRUDER is a playwright and translator who has recently turned to fiction. His stories have appeared in *The Gettysburg Review* and the *Harrington Gay Men's Fiction Quarterly*. Queer writer-hero-influences would include Forster, Purdy, Tennessee Williams, and Thornton Wilder. Favorite flower: the peony.

RICHARD McCANN's *Mother of Sorrows*, from which "The Diarist" is taken, will be published by Pantheon Books in April 2005. He is also the author of *Ghost Letters* (1994 Beatrice Hawley Award, 1994 Capricorn Poetry Award) and the editor (with Michael Klein) of *Things Shaped in Passing: More 'Poets for Life' Writing from the AIDS Pandemic*. He lives in Washington, D.C., where he teaches in the graduate program in creative writing at American University, and he serves on the Board of Trustees of the Fine Arts Work Center in Provincetown.

NOAH MICHELSON likes road trips, secret identities, horror movie monsters, and the banana level of ms. pac-man. Queer writers he is reading: "Right now Daphne Gottlieb, David Trinidad, and Cattulus." Favorite flower: Tiger Lily.

MARK MOODY lives in Baltimore where he commits social work to support his poetry habit. Queer influences include Mark Doty & Mark Wunderlich; currently reading Walt Whitman and Brian Teare. Favorite flower: the quill chrysanthemum.

HONOR MOORE is the author of *The White Blackbird: A Life of the Painter Margaret Sargent by Her Granddaughter* (1996) and three volumes of poems: *Memoir* (1988), *Darling* (2000), and *Red Shoes* (2005).

CHRISTOPHER MURRAY's poetry can be seen in the anthology *Bend, Don't Shatter* (Soft Skull Press, 2004). His poem, *I Got Beat Up A Lot In High School* was read recently by Garrison Keillor on the Writer's Almanac on NPR. Queer influence? O'Hara. Favorite flower? Anus.

JEFF OAKS teaches at the University of Pittsburgh, where he runs the Pittsburgh Contemporary Writers Series. Newest chapbook is *The Moon of Books*. Queer Influences: Auden, Rich, O'Hara, Robert Francis, Carl Phillips. Favorite flower: Sunflower.

JULIET PATTERSON lives in Minneapolis. Her work has appeared in *Verse, Conduit, DIAGRAM, The Journal, 42opus* and other publications. Queer influences: Mark Wunderlich's *Voluntary Servitude*, Carole Maso's Ava, and the letters of Emily Dickinson Favorite flower: Black-eyed Susan.

STEVEN RYDMAN recently completed his MFA at Antioch University Los Angeles. Even though they met only once, briefly at a reading, Mark Doty's presence as a poet has always provided buoys to look for in this wide and turbulent literary sea. Steven's favorite flower is the sunflower.

GREGG SHAPIRO, a 1999 inductee into Chicago's Gay and Lesbian Hall of Fame and a recipient of the 2003 Outstanding Support OMA (Outmusic Award), is a pop culture journalist, poet and fiction writer whose creative work has been published widely. Shapiro and his life partner Rick Karlin live with their dogs Dusty and k.d. in Chicago.

PEGGY SHINNER's work has appeared in *TriQuarterly, Western Humanities Review, Another Chicago Magazine*, and others. She is a recent recipient of an Illinois Arts Council Fellowship. "I owe a great deal to Virginia Woolf."

MECCA J. SULLIVAN's fiction has appeared in Columbia and Yale Universities' undergraduate journals. She loves Audre Lorde and *Birds of Paradise*, and is currently working on her first novel.

LISA VERIGIN is a freelance writer whose poetry has most recently appeared in *Tar Wolf Review* and *Diner*. She's a fan of Maureen Seaton's poetry and gardenias.

ABE LOUISE YOUNG is a poet and journalist living in Austin, Texas. Favorite flower: Southern Magnolia. Plucking one carries a hefty fine in Louisiana & so inspired her early deviant pleasures. Queer influences: Rich, Whitman, Lorde, Broumas, Doty, Bridgforth. Visit her online at www.abelouiseyoung.com.